LIFE
WITHOUT
LIMITATIONS

A Complete Guide To Overcoming Pain, Moving With Confidence, And
Maintaining Your Active Lifestyle — Regardless Of Age

D0888783

Essential Reading For Anyone Over 40 Worried About Having To Give Up
The Activities They Love

Dr. Carl Baird

LIFE
WITHOUT
LIMITATIONS

TABLE OF CONTENTS

Introduction

As we begin our journey into overcoming pain through better movement and strength, we want to remind you to keep the big picture in mind. While much of what we discuss in this book can help you overcome pain, the real goal is to improve how you experience the world around you. The healthcare world has a tendency to become so hyper-focused on pain that we forget the bigger picture. We forget that this pain really isn't the problem. The impact that this pain is having on your ability to enjoy the world around you is the real problem. Whether that be completely stopping you from taking part in the activities you love, or serving as a distraction that prevents you from 100% enjoying the things that really matter — whether that be your time with friends, family or your favorite activities.

With the big picture in mind, we have to acknowledge that the traditional approach to treating pain is not working. More than ever, people deal with the worry and concern that they may have to give up on the activities they love because of pain that has not gone away or is slowly starting to get worse. They're relying on pain pills, endless doctor visits, or costly (and sometimes debilitating) surgeries just to make it through their day. All of which provide short term relief without achieving the long-term solutions they are looking for. The problem doesn't lie in the treatments available. It lies in our overall approach.

Current methods for managing pain are designed to help you live with a problem rather than completely solving it.

This book offers a NEW approach to overcoming pain and maintaining your lifestyle that puts you in control of how you feel as you age – all while helping you grow, learn, and build confidence in your body's ability to handle the activities you love, regardless of age. This approach has been shaped by my experience in the traditional medical world. To get an understanding of its importance we should start with explaining our journey through the traditional medical system - so let's start there.

My name is Dr. Carl Baird – a chiropractor, sports therapist, movement specialist, and fitness enthusiast. One of the most common questions I get asked is how did I decide to be a chiropractor? And if I'm being honest, the answer isn't because I'm IN LOVE with chiropractic work and think it's the answer to all our pain/injury/health problems. The answer goes a bit deeper than that.

Growing up I always knew I wanted to be in the health field. My mom was a medical doctor. She went back to medical school when I was eight years old, old enough to see and understand the sacrifice it takes to get through school, complete your residency, and compete for jobs. All for the opportunity to help your community improve its health.

I also saw her gradually become frustrated with how the medical system operates and the negative impact it can have on patient care and outcomes. Hospitals setting appointment times (regardless of the number of problems someone may be experiencing). Insurance companies determining what treatments to prescribe. Despite her advanced degree, she felt like she had no control in the care that her patients received.

Feeling burned out, she eventually left the hospital system and opened a private practice offering conservative pain management services – giving her freedom and control to provide the level of care her patients needed and deserved. **It was apparent that the hospital and insurance system wasn't working for the patients OR the doctors.** Her experience in the medical system left a lasting impression on my career path and a strong belief that there HAS to be a better approach to overcoming pain.

Following graduation from chiropractic school, I spent years working in traditional chiropractic clinics, providing adjustments and soft tissue therapies to treat pain and injury. The most common pattern we saw? People feeling great when they left the office – only to have pain return days, weeks, or months later. **We served as more of a band-aid than a real solution.** Now instead of relying on pain pills, they were relying on chiropractic adjustments. I guess that's a little better – but still not the solution that most people are looking for.

And as time goes on and we start to get a bit older, what started as annoying pain becomes more frequent and intense. It starts to creep into our daily activities. We notice it at work, at outings with friends and families, and during our workouts, hikes, whatever we like to do. It becomes harder to ignore and starts to distract us from the activities we love. And the pain pills, chiropractic adjustments, or soft tissue therapies that used to work fail to bring a lasting solution that we really want. Soon we're told that there is nothing we can do. That we have a "bad back" (or knee, shoulder, hip, etc.) and that we have to deal with it. We end up feeling stuck.

This book is designed to get you unstuck. To give you control of how you feel as you age. Here are a few of the things that I hope you take away from this book:

- The real cause of pain we associate with "getting older"

- Why the traditional approach to medicine has failed to provide long term solutions to things like neck, back, shoulder, and knee pain

- The top ten myths in healthcare that are holding you back from the results you want

- The top reasons movement and strength training NEED to be a part of any treatment plan

- Movement fundamentals to get rid of neck, back, shoulder, and knee pain for good

- The most common movement mistakes that lead to chronic pain and injury

- Where to strengthen and what to stretch to protect your body from injury

- What you can do today, to be sure you can live your life without any limitations

If the above scenario sounds a bit like your situation, we encourage you to read on. The information in this book might just change your life.

Part One

The current approach to pain management isn't working. In Part One of this book we discuss a few of the reasons the traditional approach to medicine will never bring us the long-lasting solutions we are looking for, and we also introduce you to the concept of how deficiencies in movement and strength contribute to the pain we experience as we age.

We end by showing you how adding a movement and strength training program to your care plan is what you need to provide LASTING solutions to your pain and injury issues so you can live your life without any limitations.

Chapter One

THE ROLE OF MOVEMENT AND STRENGTH IN AGE-RELATED PAIN

One of the most damaging beliefs in the healthcare world is the belief that pain is a natural byproduct of getting older: the idea that after we hit a certain age, pain is just something we have to live with. The worst part is this belief is purveyed by doctors when they can't figure out the "cause" of a patient's pain. They convince people that they have a "bad back" or "bad knees" and that it is something they just have to live with.

This leads to the belief that there's nothing we can do. That we're stuck. That we're doomed to a life of pain simply because we're older than we were five years ago. The good news is this is 100% not true. In this chapter we'll take a look at the REAL cause of the pain we associate with getting older.

The Real Cause of Age-Related Pain

You'll probably hear me repeat this over 100 times in this book: pain is not part of getting older. Pain as we age is caused by one of two things: either we're not moving enough, or in the case of the active individual, we're moving too often with inadequate form or inadequate strength to support the body. Both of these scenarios lead to small irritations that will ALWAYS catch up to us. To repeat: it's not the fact that we're older that has led to our back/knee/shoulder pain. **It's these repeated, small** irritations compounded over time that are the cause of the pain we associate with age.

These small irritations come in the form of altered movement patterns that consistently load tissues until failure. While it may look like the pain or injury came "all of a sudden," the truth is that it has been building up for months (and most likely years). To understand what we mean in simpler terms we can use the following equation:

Poor Movement x Time (Age) = Pain

Looking at this equation you can see that while time is a contributing factor (the longer we allow these small irritations to go on, the worse they get), it is NOT the cause. **The cause is the poor movement.** This is important to understand because we can't control our age. We <u>can</u> control our movement. And the focus of this book will teach you how to move in a way that allows you to live your life without limitations – regardless of age.

Is Your Low Back Pain a Low Back Problem? (And Other Conditions...)

When building a plan to overcome pain it's vital that we go beyond the surface level. The common thinking is, "My low back hurts, so why don't we just treat my low back and I'll get better?" This can help provide short-term relief but won't result in the long-term solution we're looking for.

To create a long-term solution, we need to build an understanding of why the low back is being loaded beyond its capacity. To do this we need to understand that aside from major traumas, <u>our back pain</u> (hip, knee, shoulder, etc.) <u>is not a back issue</u>. Instead, it's a movement issue that is leading to low back pain. Either we aren't coordinating our movements in the right way (which leads to excess load on our spine), we don't have the functional strength to support the activities we're performing, or we're too stiff and our body is forced to compensate to get in the proper position (more on all this later).

"Move Well. Then Move Often."

That is the universal motto (created by our friends over at Functional Movement Systems) for manual therapy and movement specialists to help clients avoid the pain we associate with getting older. The idea is that before we go crazy in the gym or other activities, we need to learn how to move in a way to protect our bodies.

Injuries come when we skip the first step of the motto: when we ignore the "Move Well" and jump right into the "Move Often." Without the foundation for what proper movement should look like — and more importantly, FEEL like — we are setting ourselves up for pain and injury later on down the line.

What Does It Mean to Move Well?

Learning how to move well isn't as sexy as burning off steam at the gym or going hiking, mountain biking, running — whatever it is that you LOVE to do. But it is what is required if you want to spare your joints and continue to do what you love without any limitations. As we start to focus on improving movement to prevent age-related pain there are three things we need to address:

Movement Patterning

Movement patterns are how our body coordinates movements to perform basic tasks. How we lift something off the ground, how we reach overhead, and how we walk/run/jump are all examples of movement patterning. Movement Patterning is about improving our body awareness. Creating an understanding of what movement should look like – and more importantly, FEEL like – so we can be sure we're loading our joints in a way to avoid injury and engaging the correct muscles to avoid compensation patterns that may put extra stress on our bodies.

Functional Strength

By functional strength we mean developing adequate strength to perform your activities of daily living. This means it's different for each individual. Avoiding pain and injury as we age requires that our body has the necessary strength to support our body and protect our joints.

Mobility

It's also imperative that our joints can go through their full range of motion. Mobility in our context means an ability to move freely and without restriction. Limitations in movements cause compensation patterns that place our body in vulnerable positions and lead to pain and injury. We'll cover this idea in more detail later.

The Fundamental Five Movements

Simply asking someone to "improve their movement" isn't very helpful. There is no cookie-cutter approach to improving movement because every hobby and activity has its own requirements. How do we know where we should start? <u>Movement is built on basic, fundamental principles.</u> Developing an understanding and ability to perform, strengthen, and master the following five movements creates results that carry over into any activity you choose to perform:

Breath

One of the most important and most commonly overlooked movement patterns is our breath: a movement we perform over 20,000 times a day. Improving our breathing mechanics can save us from years of neck pain, back pain, and headaches and can even reduce stress and improve our cardiovascular and digestive functions.

Hinge/Lift

The hip hinge and lift are THE foundational movements on which all other movements are built upon, which is why it's important to spend time creating a better understanding of what the movement should look and feel like. Having a basic understanding of how to bend forward and lift from the ground can save you from years of pain.

Squat

The squat is the most important of the full-body movements. To perform properly requires good movement patterning as well as adequate mobility and strength. By identifying and correcting dysfunctions in our overhead squat we can improve the efficiency of any movement.

Lunge

The lunge is one of the most "functional" movements — meaning that it most readily translates to real-world activities. Walking, running, hiking, and jumping all require the same muscle groups that we train with lunges. Improving our lunge will build resilient lower bodies that will help you recover from ANY lower extremity (hip, knee, ankle, foot) injury.

Push/Pull/Press

These are actually three separate movements that are required to create balance and improve overall shoulder health. By focusing on improving functional movements of the shoulder rather than trying to strengthen isolated muscles of the rotator cuff, we can create solutions that carry over into the real world.

By improving our understanding of how to properly perform these five movements, we can carry that knowledge over into whatever activity you choose. In Part Two of this book we'll look at ways we can specifically improve each of these movement patterns.

Do You Have a Movement Problem?

How can we tell if you have a movement problem that needs to be addressed? For most people, it's easy to tell before we lay a hand on them or even watch them move. There are five tell-tale signs of a movement issue that we look for before working with anyone, and we'll outline them here:

1. Previous Injury
   "After an injury, tissues heal, but the muscles learn, they readily develop habits of guarding that outlast the injury." — Functional Training Handbook
   The number-one risk factor for a future injury is a previous injury. Any trauma, no matter how big or small, causes changes

in our joints, muscles, and nervous system, which alter the way we move and increase the likelihood of suffering another injury.

2. **Recurring Pain**

    Treating an injury without correcting the cause (the movement patterns) increases the likelihood of suffering a relapse. If you have experienced similar pain more than once, you most likely have a movement issue that needs to be addressed.

3. **Gradual Onset Pain**

    Pain from movement deficiencies usually cannot be pinned down to one specific incident. The majority of injuries are the result of excessive loads from altered movement patterns that gradually and progressively reduce a tissue's tolerance until failure.

4. **Sedentary Lifestyle**

    Our bodies are constantly adapting to the stresses we put on them. Increased hours of sitting and other sedentary postures cause changes in our muscles that create imbalances in the way we move, altering the way we load our joints and, over time, leading to pain and injury.

5. **Limited Range of Motion**

    Can you touch your toes? Can you squat so your thighs get to parallel with the floor? Can you touch your hands behind your back? Missing range of motion is a common contributor to the pain we associate with getting older. Inabilities to touch our toes or get into a good squat position are signs that we lack the mobility to properly load our joints throughout the day.

Why Movement Matters

The conventional approach to treating pain is not working. More and more people are relying on pain pills, endless chiropractic visits and other therapies, or costly (and sometimes debilitating) surgeries in the hope of solving their pain. We're here to tell you that the solution to our pain problem is already here and it won't be found inside a traditional doctor's office. Because it lies in the way we move. It lies in our body's ability to support the activities we love.

If we keep trying the same things over and over again, we're going to keep getting the same results. Throughout the course of this book we hope to show you how improper movement leads to the pain we associate with getting older, and we hope to convince you that movement and strength training are NEEDED to truly overcome pain and live our lives without limitations.

Chapter Two

What if our entire approach to treating pain and improving health is wrong? The reason people are living with pain for longer than they should isn't because the drugs and treatments available aren't effective, but because our entire approach is designed to create short-term relief without providing any long-term solutions.

Here's the truth if you're serious about staying active and strong and living your life without any limitations: you don't need more pain pills, and that new "minimally invasive" surgery won't be the answer. The answer to overcoming pain and living our lives without limitation will only be found through a fundamental shift in how we approach getting out of pain. In this chapter we take a look at the flaws with the traditional approach to medicine and what we can do to fix them.

Placing the Emphasis on Doctors Over Patients

The traditional medical system has placed so much importance on the doctors, treatments, and technologies that we've forgotten about the most important part of the treatment plan: the patient. The current medical system promotes the idea that someone or something can "fix" us. We've been programmed since we were kids to go to the doctor when something goes wrong, and he or she will put us back together.

This works for traumatic injuries or illnesses. It doesn't work for pain. Why? Because there isn't a pill, chiropractic adjustment, acupuncture treatment, or massage that can improve years of poor movement patterns or inadequate strength. Remember, the number one cause of age-related pain is poor movement patterns that have been compounded over time — wearing down our joints, muscles, and tendons until they eventually fail.

A better approach is one that puts the focus back on the patient. An approach that places LESS reliance on doctors, treatments, and technologies and instead build confidence and foster self-reliance in the individual. An approach that understands that there is no pill, treatment or technology that will ever be able to improve movement or strength. This doesn't mean that doctors aren't important; it does mean that their role has to change. Instead of simply being someone who provides a diagnosis, writes a prescription, and performs a treatment, they have to transition to be an educator, a coach, a motivator. It's a more human approach, and it's what is needed if we're serious about overcoming pain and injury.

Take-Home Message: You are the most important part of your treatment plan. Any plan to overcome pain and improve health must incorporate you as the primary component.

Focusing on Services Over Solutions

Taking a quick look at your typical doctor, chiropractor, or physical therapist's website, you will most likely see a full list of their services. Chiropractic adjustments. Cupping. Instrument assisted soft tissue massage. Some clinics even call their physicians "service providers." We've been taught that these services can "fix" us, and so it is what most clinics want to promote. The problem? A chiropractic adjustment or one-hour massage alone will never undo years of poor movement patterns or inadequate strength. Services provide short-term, symptomatic relief when <u>what we really want are long-term solutions to our pain</u>.

The focus on services runs DEEP in the traditional medical system. Insurance companies reimburse clinics for services they render. They don't concern themselves if the services solved the patient's problem or the impact they have on patients' real lives. The result is that clinics are forced to simply provide stand-alone services and can't spend the time to create a comprehensive plan to SOLVE the issue and improve the patient's quality of life. You know — what ACTUALLY matters.

If you've been to a traditional chiropractor or physical therapist's office, you've probably experienced this yourself. Being led to a table with some heat and electronic stimulation. Led to a doctor where an adjustment and some massage are performed. And then told to come back every two days until the pain goes away. You may feel good for a few days, weeks, or months, but the pain eventually comes back. (Remember the idea of short-term relief vs. long-term solutions?)

A better approach is to create plans that offer solutions: an approach that combines the benefits of these services to promote and speed healing with a comprehensive plan to actually solve the problem. This approach takes into account things like movement patterns, functional strength deficiencies, and lifestyle factors and puts them into an actionable plan designed to help patients achieve real-world solutions to their pain and injuries.

Take-Home Message: Services help you live with a problem. Solutions alleviate the problem.

Placing Emphasis on Passive Therapies

This is an idea that goes hand in hand with our reliance on services rather than creating solutions. When we say "passive therapies," we mean any therapy where we passively lie on the table and receive treatment. While we're coming to understand that age-related pain is the result of poor movement patterns compounded over time, we're still trying to rely on these passive therapies to treat movement and strength problems. No wonder it isn't working. The only way to improve movement is to move. A better approach is one that uses active, movement-based therapies to get patients engaged rather than simply being passive bystanders in their care.

Take-Home Message: Passive therapies will never solve movement and strength issues and thus will fail to provide long-term solutions to age-related pain.

Focusing on Isolated Body Parts

The traditional approach to back pain? Let's treat the low back. Hip pain? Then let's treat the hip. **The truth is that pain and injuries never occur in isolation.** Aside from major traumas, your back pain isn't a back issue. There's a term in the movement and manual therapy world we call "regional interdependence". The term refers to the concept that seemingly unrelated impairments in a remote anatomical region can contribute to or be associated with a patient's primary complaint.

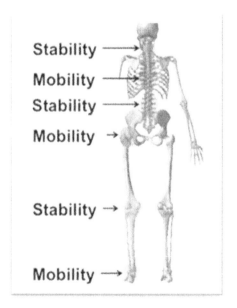

One way to look at this relationship is through the lens of alternating mobile and stable joints. You can see how this alternating pattern can explain how many injuries occur. Let's use low back pain as an example. In general, we want our lower back to be stable and strong to prevent excess movement on our joints and discs. What happens if we see limitations in our hip and mid back? Two areas that we want to be more mobile and less stiff? The consequence is that the low back will sacrifice some of its stability to obtain the full range of motion caused by tight hips and the mid back. It's this abnormal motion in the low back that is one of the primary reasons for injuries to the discs and joints of the low back.

While the pain shows up in the low back, the real cause is the lack of movement in our hips and mid back. If all we do is hammer away at the low back for three weeks, which is what the traditional medical system would have us do, we will most likely experience short term relief without the long-term solutions that we really want. A better approach is one that looks at the entire body, how you coordinate movements, and aims to improve full body motion and strength.

Take-Home Message: Pain and injury never occur in isolation. A full-body approach is required to find long lasting results.

Ignoring Lifestyle Factors

The traditional approach to medicine almost completely ignores lifestyle factors as a contributor into the pain we experience. Even as a chiropractor and sports therapist, it's easy to get wrapped up in the physical aspect of pain. That because it's our back/knee/shoulder that is injured that we only need to address the back/knee/shoulder to get out of pain. While movement and manual therapy is important in helping the body heal, it will be short lived if we're dealing with chronic stress and poor sleeping and eating patterns. Science is showing that lifestyle factors play a HUGE role in the amount of pain we experience. We'll discuss three of the top lifestyle factors that contribute to the pain we experience while getting older.

1. Nutrition

    Chronic inflammation can predispose our bodies to chronic pain. Eating diets high in sugar and processed foods contribute to inflammation that sensitizes our pain receptors and thus leads to chronic pain. Eating more fruits, vegetables, nuts, and healthy fats decreases the inflammation in our bodies and can help decrease the pain we experience.

2. Stress

    Studies have shown that increased levels of stress contribute to the pain we experience on a daily basis. Daily meditation has been shown to decrease stress levels in the body and can be useful in easing chronic pain.

3. Sleep

    Sleep impacts pain. You may have noticed when you sleep poorly and are tired, your pain tends to be worse. Studies have shown that one of the most important predictors of pain intensity is the number of hours slept the night before.

A better approach takes a holistic attitude to overcoming pain. An approach that includes improved nutrition, stress, and sleep habits that not only treat pain but carry over into every aspect of our lives — from our relationships to our work and to our overall quality of life.

Take-Home Message: Pain can be impacted by all aspects of our lives, not simply the physical damage to an injured tissue.

Treating Pain as the CAUSE

"To reduce pain, we need to reduce the credible evidence of danger and increase credible evidence of safety." — Lorimer Moseley

Pain is a symptom, not a diagnosis. It is also one of the easiest symptoms to manipulate. Does your left shoulder hurt? I bet if I punched you in the right shoulder, the left shoulder would hurt less. It's that easy!

You're going to have to bear with me as I nerd out for a bit here, but this is an important concept to understanding how movement and strength programming can help you live your life without limitations. We're talking pain science. The thing about pain science is that it's always changing. The more we understand about how our brain creates and interprets pain, the better we can treat and manage acute and chronic pain.

Traditional pain science has suggested that pain comes from the bottom up. This means if we suffer an injury to a certain area of our body, that area of the body then tells the brain that we're in pain. This makes sense for traumatic and acute injuries. If we fall down the stairs and land on our back, the joints and muscles in our back send the signal to our brain to let us know about the injury and to protect that area of the body while it heals.

But what about pain that has stayed for months or years without a significant injury? **The tissue (joints, muscles, tendons, ligaments, etc.) in your body have healed, but you're still experiencing pain. What gives?**

New pain science is showing that the sensation of pain (especially pain that has lasted for more than three months) can also come from the top down. Our brain creates the pain sensation to inform us of a perceived threat to our body so that we avoid further aggravation or injury. That is good for an acute injury but becomes a problem if that messaging continues to be sent even after the tissue has healed.

A better approach to overcoming pain takes into account that sometimes our brain interprets a threat that really isn't there. And what's needed isn't more manual therapy, but an exercise and strength program to convince the brain that there is no longer a threat and it's OK to move that area of the body.

Take Home Message: Building confidence in our body's ability to handle our daily activities is needed to overcome pain.

Symptom Management Over Real-World Goals

The traditional medical system has a habit of being hyper-focused on treating symptoms. You have back pain? Then we need to get rid of the back pain at all cost – with no consideration of anything else. Here's a bunch of pain pills; they will take your back pain away – and completely destroy your liver and kidneys! Or how about this? We fuse your spine so you stop irritating the injured disc – but you may never be able to play basketball, lift your grandkids, or sit comfortably for longer than one hour. Doesn't that sound great?

By focusing so intensely on the symptoms we miss the big picture. Healthcare should be about improving how we experience the world around us. How we utilize the tools we were given to do what makes us happy. It includes different lifestyles and body types while requiring the adoption of the lifestyle changes necessary to avoid the chronic illness and injury that could limit our ability to do what we love.

What does this mean for healthcare? It means that true health will never be found inside a doctor's office (unless your passion is sitting in a waiting room). Our focus needs to shift from treating symptoms to finding ways to improve how we experience the world around us. To working towards creating the optimum conditions to achieve happiness.

A better approach keeps the big picture in mind. Understanding that pain isn't the problem; the impact the pain is having on your ability to do what you love is what matters. As such, the overall purpose of the treatment plan shouldn't be only to decrease pain, but to get you back to doing what you love.

Take Home Message: By keeping the big picture in mind we can create results that not only take away pain but carry over into what's important in your world.

An Over-Reliance on Evidence

You're going to have to bear with me on this one because it goes against everything we've been taught. Isn't evidence-based medicine good? Don't we want our treatments backed by solid research? And the answer is yes – but we don't want our over reliance on research to stop us from taking action that we KNOW works. I don't need a 50,000 participant, 10-year study to tell me that taking steps to improve movement, strength, nutrition, and growth will resolve a lot of my issues.

The real limitation that evidence-based medicine has in the real world is its promotion of inactivity. Focusing on studying single variables (like pain) suggests that we will someday find a single cure. And until we find that single cure there is nothing we can do.

We get caught in the mindset that we can't do anything because we don't yet know everything.

Conflicting research through easily manipulated studies leads to public confusion, which further spurs inactivity. It's easy to dismiss results of these specific studies because they are so specific that they "don't apply to me." The real issue with our chronic health issues is that it's this inactivity in our younger years that is causing the chronic medical problems we see later in life.

I want to emphasize that I'm not suggesting we no longer need science and research in the medical world. What I am suggesting is that our reliance on science and research can blind us to solutions that are available to us now and work in the real world. It furthers our dependence on treatments and technologies rather than actions that we know are effective. We can't continue to rely solely on research at the expense of common sense. Remember, our actions are compounded over time. Good decisions lead to better results over time. Negative actions lead to negative results over time. Positive actions lead to positive results. This is why we have to take action now, even if we don't have the scientific proof, and the sooner the better.

Putting It All Together

I hope by now you can see some of the inherent flaws in the traditional approach to treating pain and why some of the therapies you have tried haven't provided you the solution you were looking for. And I also hope you are gathering some hope that pain is not a natural byproduct of getting older. By simply changing our approach, not the therapies, we can control how we feel as we age. By placing more focus on the individual, we can create self-reliance rather than a dependency on doctors and other passive therapies. By treating pain from a more holistic lens that incorporates movement, strength, and lifestyle factors we can create SOLUTIONS to our pain problems rather than simply helping you live with the problem. By focusing on the big picture, we can create results that matter to the patient – helping them do what they love and living their life without limitations.

I bet at this point you're wondering, "But will this approach work for me?" Without knowing a single thing about you and your story, I can without a doubt say "YES." And I can say it with 100% confidence. How can I do that?

Because I know that there is no instance where improving movement and strength will not be beneficial in SOME aspect of your life. Adopting a mindset of continual growth, learning, and confidence will invariably make you a better person and improve the quality of your life.

Chapter Three

Before we get into ways to improve movement, it's important that we address many of the false beliefs that are so prevalent in the pain and injury world. Each of the topics we cover in this chapter are ideas that we have heard from actual patients. Things that their doctors, family, and friends have repeated to the point that they accept them as fact.

False beliefs are what keep us stuck. When these false beliefs are accepted as fact, they keep us from taking any action to improve our health because they give the idea that there's nothing we can do. In this chapter we want to address some of the most common false beliefs we hear from patients in the clinic and provide some clarity that will get you unstuck and on a path to better movement and health and to keep you doing what you love.

False Belief #1: Pain Is Just Part of Getting Older

We hope this one is obvious by now. Pain is not a natural byproduct of getting older. Any pain that we experience as we age is the result of small irritations repeated over a long period of time. **Small irritations caused by improper movement.** An inability to coordinate our movements through basic movement patterns, resulting in loading joints that weren't meant to take such a beating. A lack of functional strength necessary to protect our joints, muscles, and ligaments during our daily activities. And missing mobility that leads to compensation patterns elsewhere in the body that eventually break down and lead to pain and injury.

The central goal of this book is to put you back in the driver's seat when it comes to how you feel as you age. It's so important to dispel the myth that pain is part of getting older because we cannot control our age. We can control our movement. If we accept pain as part of getting older, we end up in the mindset that there's nothing we can do, so we end up doing nothing, and the pain gets worse, and the myth gets further engrained. A vicious cycle that leads many to give up the activities they love.

False Belief #2: Arthritis Is the Cause of Your Pain

We hear this one A LOT. A patient went to their doctor and got X-rays. The X-rays showed degeneration or arthritis in their spine, and the doctor concluded that their arthritis is the source of their pain. Here's the truth: degeneration on X-rays is extremely common in anyone over 30 and is not the cause of your pain. Most people over 30 have some form of degeneration in their joints and experience no pain. On the other side, there are many people who have lots of pain – and their X-rays show no degeneration.

This idea is backed up in the research. A recent systematic review (summation of multiple studies on the topic) concluded, "Imaging findings of spine degeneration are present in high proportions of asymptomatic (no pain) individuals, increasing with age. Many imaging-based degenerative features are likely part of normal aging and unassociated with pain."

In fact, they found that even a third of people in their 20s had some form of degeneration (arthritis). Here's a breakdown of the percentage of people studied who had some form of arthritis with no physical pain:

- People in their 20s – 37%
- People in their 30s – 52%
- People in their 40s – 68%
- People in their 50s – 80%
- People in their 60s – 88%
- People in their 70s – 93%
- People in their 80s – 96%

What to take away from these numbers? Some level of arthritis is common (even in younger populations) in people with no pain — meaning that arthritis is not the CAUSE of pain.

Source: Brinjikji W, Luetmer PH, Comstock B, et al. Systematic literature review of imaging features of spinal degeneration in asymptomatic populations. AJNR Am J Neuroradiol. 2014;36(4):811–816. doi:10.3174/ajnr.A4173

False Belief #3: Bulging Discs Are the Cause of My Pain

Taking it a step further, many of our clients have opted for an MRI that has shown they have a "disc bulge" and have been told that this bulge is the cause of their pain. Just like the X-ray, the presence of a disc bulge in the spine has no correlation with the amount of pain we experience. It's 100% possible to have a disc bulge and have no pain. It's also 100% possible to have back pain with no disc bulge. Just like with the X-rays, studies have shown that MRI findings were not related to the intensity of pain and do not explain the cause of a patient's pain.

Worse yet, studies have shown there is so much variability in MRI reading among radiologists that where you have your MRI read will have significant impact on your diagnosis and the type of treatment you receive.

There are plenty of instances where imaging is needed and necessary. Chronic and age-related pain is not one of them. The finding of an X-ray or MRI rarely identifies the cause of such pain, and placing too much emphasis on them damages patients' expectations and has a negative impact on how they recover.

False Belief #4: Surgery Is My Only Option

Another major issue with these image findings is they are then used as justification to get patients under the knife. Spinal degeneration? Let's just fuse everything together. If we can't move, we will stop irritating our tissues, right? Knee arthritis? Let's go in there and "clean it up." Bulging disc? Let's go in there and take out the injured part of the disc — that should do the trick.

Stuart McGill, the leading expert on treating back pain (and who has a PhD in treating low back pain), states in his book, *Back Mechanic: The Secret to a Healthy Spine Your Doctor Isn't Telling You*, that 95% of the patients he sees DO NOT need surgery, even though many were told it was their only cure. He explains that surgeries often work in the short term, but studies have shown that after a few years a surgical patient's status is comparable to those who chose the non-surgical option. One reason is that surgery doesn't correct (and also contributes to) the underlying movement and strength deficiencies that lead to tissue breakdown and pain. Beginning to see a pattern here?

Another thing to consider when you're looking into surgery is that it truly is an "all in" approach. You're not just "fixing" the injured area; you're cutting though muscles and nerves, you're removing areas of bone or cartilage that does not grow back, and you're starting a scarring process that can entrap nerves and lead to chronic pain. Basically, there's no going back from surgery. It's an expensive and potentially debilitating treatment option whose long-term effectiveness has yet to be proven. Is that really a risk you want to take with your life?

False Belief #5: Pain Runs in the Family

I'm not sure where this belief started but it is one of the most common things we hear when we start working with clients. My mom had a "bad back" which means I'm doomed to suffer the same fate. My dad needed shoulder surgery so I've got "bad shoulders" and will probably need shoulder surgery as well. This is a belief that keeps orthopedic surgeons in business but one that has no basis in reality. Pain is not genetic. Now, you and your family may share similar lifestyles that contribute to the pain you experience as you age, but by improving movement and strength you won't be destined to suffer the same fate as your parents, aunts, uncles, or anyone else in your family.

False Belief #6: I Will Rest and Wait for the Pain to Go Away

For many, the go-to response for pain and injury (often told to them by their doctor) is to rest and take some pain pills and wait for the pain to go away on its own. And while the pain may go away for a bit, it always comes back and is usually much worse than the first instance.

For years we've been booting, bracing, and crutching new injuries as a way to protect the area until pain self-resolves. Recent evidence suggests that prolonged immobilization not only slows healing but increases the chances of future complications. Research also shows that getting an injury moving (in a pain-free range) is the best way to speed the healing process and prevent future injuries.

Here are the top five reasons to use motion, rather than immobilization, when treating a new injury:

1. Pain free range of motion promotes the proper healing of soft tissues, which decreases the amount of scar tissue build-up in the healing process. This leads to greater range of motion and decreased chance of suffering the same injury later.
2. Even small amplitude oscillatory movements can be used to stimulate the receptors that override pain signals to the brain.
3. Joint motion stimulates the movement of synovial fluid (a lubricating fluid in our joints), which brings nutrients to the cartilage of the joint surfaces.

4. Prolonged immobilization causes joint cartilage to deteriorate, contributing to arthritis and further joint pain as we age.

5. Contraction of surrounding musculature helps pump waste products from the injury site out through our lymphatic system, limiting the amount of swelling and speeding the healing process.

The best thing you can do after suffering an injury is to get it moving. Immobilization of the injured area can lead to further damage, while movement improves the health of the tissue, speeds healing time, and protects our body from future injuries.

False Belief #7: I've Tried Physical Therapy and it Hasn't Worked

This is one of the biggest reasons people are skeptical to start a care plan at the clinic. And we 100% understand. You've already committed time and money to chiropractic or physical therapy, and it maybe felt good for a few weeks or months – but the pain came back. This goes back to Chapter Two and the idea that maybe it's not the physical therapy that failed but instead the overall approach.

Here are some questions I would ask about your previous clinic experiences. What was the overall goal, pain relief or getting you back to the activities you love? Were you given a cookie-cutter exercise plan or one that was specifically created to help you reach your goals? Were they treating the location of the pain or the cause? Were you given full-body, movement exercises or did they stick strictly to one isolated region? Were you given the time of day to ask questions and feel like you are the number-one priority? These are all questions that matter if a smooth, successful, and enjoyable recovery is to be achieved.

The problem with a lot of "old school" physical therapy clinics is they are based in the antiquated approach that focuses on providing short-term relief without spending the time to find the long-term solutions. While one clinic may have not been the right fit for you, there's a therapist that may be more appropriate for you. One that specializes in getting you back to activities you love and helping you live your life without limitations.

False Belief #8: I've Seen Some Stretches on YouTube That Have Helped

We live in the information age. We have the ability to go on YouTube and Instagram and find stretches or exercises to try to ease our pain. While there are some benefits to information being so available, there are also a few drawbacks. The first is that it gives a platform for someone with very limited real-world experience to pose as an "expert" and give bad or counterproductive advice. The second is that it gives people hope that this stretch or exercise will be the "fix" without knowing the specific conditions that are leading to your pain. Lastly, there is no cookie cutter approach to improving movement and strength. Your passions and goals for your life are unique to you and any treatment plan needs to reflect that. Trying to plug in random exercises from your favorite YouTube star won't equate with a structured plan designed to get you back to the gym, on the golf course, or on the trails (whatever it is you like to do).

False Belief #9: I'm Out of Alignment and Need to Be Put Back into Alignment

This is a myth that's more common in chiropractic circles but one that drives us crazy. Patients have been told by their chiropractor, family member, or friend that their joints are out of alignment. They come into the clinic under the assumption that something is "out" and want it to be put back "in." The truth is there's no such thing as being out of alignment. And there's no such thing as a doctor or chiropractor being able to put you back in alignment. Any sensation of being out of place would be caused by a lack of strength that leads to an inability to hold our bodies in the proper position.

False Belief #10: This New Therapy Will Fix Me

Every day our clinic is bombarded with advertisements for the next back pain cure. Our clients come from a world where they have access to YouTube "experts" and infomercials selling a "quick fix" to back pain.

There are a few problems with this line of thinking. First, it keeps our health out of our control. Only this doctor or product or therapy can fix me, so there's nothing I can currently do. Second, it keeps people from taking action. Thinking that we will someday find a single cure to back pain keeps people stuck. And lastly, it doesn't work. As we've discussed, pain is multifactorial. We will never find a treatment that improves movement and strength to remove the small irritations that lead to tissue breakdown, improves sleep and stress, has been shown to help with pain, and also gives your body the anti-inflammatory nutrients it needs to desensitize your nerves for less pain.

Here's the truth: a cure to back pain is not right around the corner. The cure is here — right here — in how we move, in how strong we are. When you understand this fact, the pain you experience is no longer a mystery. Our entire pain epidemic comes down to small improper movements that are compounded daily until our body gives up. There will be no new therapy that will magically fix you. The earlier you get started improving movement and strength, the less limitations you will have later in life.

Putting It All Together

When we look at all these false beliefs together, a pattern starts to emerge. They create an idea that the pain we experience is out of our control and we need someone or something to fix us. An approach that keeps doctors, orthopedic surgeons, and chiropractors/physical therapists very busy but still leaves patients limited in the activities they love. We hope to offer you a better approach, and that's what this book is all about. An approach that creates confidence and inspires hope that you do not have to be limited in the activities you love as you get older. One that gives you control of how you feel as you age.

One that keeps the big picture in mind by keeping the focus on allowing you to do what you love. We all have the ability to create the future we envision. Let's get after it!

Chapter Four:

WHY MOVEMENT AND STRENGTH TRAINING NEED TO
BE PART OF YOUR HEALTHCARE PLAN

In Chapter One we discussed the cause of most pain that limits our activities and keeps us from doing what we love. We learned that poor movement and strength deficiencies cause small irritations to our joints and muscles that get worse with time. And if we don't aim to improve our movement patterns, strength, and mobility, we will be doomed to give up on the activities that bring us so much joy.

In this chapter we'll discuss the benefits of adding a movement and strength program to your current healthcare routine that will help you stay active, strong, and doing what you love.

Reason #1 – Removing the Irritations (Improving Movement Patterning)

The body has an amazing ability to heal itself. However, it's unrealistic to expect the body to heal if we keep repeating the irritating activity. It's similar to "picking a scab." Each time we repeat the irritating activity, the healing process has to start all over again. If we keep repeating the wrong movement patterns, we'll never be able to fully recover from pain.

As a reminder, movement patterns are defined as the way we coordinate movements to perform basic, functional activities. How do you bend forward? How do you lift something off the ground? How do you walk, jump, run?

Improving movement patterning ensures that the loads we experience while performing our daily and weekend routines are going through joints that were meant to take on such loads. An easy example: as humans, we evolved to be bipedal creatures (walking on two feet vs. four). As such, our hips are meant to be our load-bearing and power generating joints. Flawed movement patterns change the way we load our joints, often taking loads off our hips and onto our knees, ankles, feet, or spine. For most, that's not a huge deal in the short term; when repeated over a long period of time, this always leads to pain and injury. Remember our equation:

Poor Movement x Time (Age) = Pain

The longer we go without correcting these movement patterns, the more load we put on joints that weren't meant to be handling repeated loads and the higher risk we have for dealing with pain as we age. Similar to a cut on our skin, our bodies are always trying to heal themselves. When we repeat harmful movement patterns we are essentially "picking the scab" and prolonging the healing process — which is why movement and strength programming are 100% necessary to the healing process.

Reason #2 – Protecting Our Joints (Improving Functional Strength)

Our muscles are the most important stabilizers of the body. When we perform our daily activities, we want muscles to take on most of the load.

When we aren't strong enough to handle certain activities, those forces are transferred to our more "passive" stabilizers (tendons, ligaments, joints) and that is when pain and injury occur. In the knee, if the muscles aren't strong enough to handle side-to-side movements, those forces are transferred to the ACL, LCL, and MCL and can lead to a sprain or tear.

In the spine, if we aren't strong enough to lift 50 pounds off the floor, the force goes through our intervertebral disc and leads to injury.

Adding strength training to the treatment plan doesn't mean we all need to be body-builders and in the gym 24/7. But you DO have to be strong enough to handle the activities specific to YOUR daily and weekend routines. It's 100% individual and is the reason a cookie-cutter exercise plan won't work for most people. Sit at a desk for eight hours a day? Your postural muscles need to be strong enough to prevent your head and spine from falling forward. Stay-at-home mom? You need to be strong enough to get the kids in and out of the car and perform household duties. Professional athlete? Just a tiny bit more may be required.

The point is that to prevent pain and injury as you age, your body needs to be strong enough to support itself as you perform the movements important to YOU. And because muscle loss is a natural by-product of aging, it is imperative that strength training be part of your treatment plan.

Reason #3 – Improving Mobility

Mobility (in the physical sense) is defined as the ability to move freely without restriction. If we become too stiff, we develop something called "compensation patterns." Our bodies are smart. When we're limited in how we move, our body will compensate to perform the task at hand. In order to get the extra depth in a squat, we'll round our pelvis to get the extra range of motion – putting our spine in a bad spot. These compensation patterns occur after an injury to protect an area (e.g. limping after a sprained ankle) or when physical limitations prevent a joint from going through its full range of motion. While this may seem like a great solution to mobility issues there is one major problem:

Compensation patterns only work for so long before something breaks down.

To achieve full movement in a joint that is stiff, we often have to sacrifice stability elsewhere. This causes wear and tear on joints and tissues. As we've learned, while you won't experience pain right away, the more miles you accumulate with these compensations the more likely you'll experience pain and dysfunction as well as increase the probability of experiencing a more serious injury later on down the road.

Reason #4 – Improving Motor Control

How well does your brain communicate with your body? Motor control is defined as the process by which humans and animals use their brain/cognition to activate and coordinate the muscles and limbs involved in the performance of a motor skill. This skill is often lost due to the sedentary nature of our lifestyle. Proper motor control is vital to preventing injury as it ensures the correct timing of muscle contractions.

Want to have some fun? Test your motor control with these two easy exercises:

1. **Glute Squeeze and Release**

- Perform Lying on Back
- Squeeze glute (butt muscles) as hard as you can
- Slowly remove tension from right cheek
- Slowly remove tension from left cheek
- Slowly contract right cheek
- Slowly contract left cheek
- Slowly release both at the same time
- Continue routine for one minute

How good is your control? Is it a smooth release from contraction? Jerky? Can you release one side while maintaining contraction in the other? To many people (especially those who sit for long hours) this exercise can be much more difficult than it appears.

2. **Toe Control**

- Perform While Standing
- Lift your big toe while keeping other toes in place.
- Lift your other four toes while keeping big toe in place
- Splay toes apart.

How'd you do? If you struggled with these exercises you can always improve through practice and repetition. Movement and strength training help us to control our movements and be sure that our muscles engage when we need them to avoid further injuring our bodies.

Reason #5 – Improving Confidence

How we move impacts every aspect of our life. From the pain we experience to how we interact with our friends and coworkers to the amount of joy we get from the activities we love. Think about someone you view as very confident: How do they move? What's their posture like? The most important reason for including movement and strength training into the healthcare world is confidence it brings: the confidence to handle the activities we love, the confidence to try new things, the confidence to be ourselves.

After an injury, many people develop a phenomenon called fear avoidance behaviors. These are behaviors that patients adapt that involve avoiding certain movements and activities for fear that they'll be painful. This leads to compensatory movements which only serve to prolong recovery. Remember, the number-one cause of a future injury is a previous injury. Years after the injury, the healing has taken place but the thoughts and feelings surrounding the injury still remain and people are hesitant to try new things. Movement and strength training improve a patient's confidence and trust in their body's ability to handle their activities of daily living.

While pain reduction and faster healing are primary goals of any treatment plan, restoring confidence and trust in our body through a strength training program is vital for long-term recovery as well as how we interact with those around us.

Reason #6: Building Self-Reliance

The unfortunate truth is that health and longevity will never be found in a doctor's office. An hour a week at your doctor will never outweigh the 167 hours we spend in the real world. This is why if we're serious about finding long-term solutions to our pain problems, incorporating movement and strength training is a necessity. We can't watch the way you move in the gym. We can't go with you on a run to correct your form. We need to help clients build an understanding of what movement should look like – and more importantly FEEL like – so they can stop relying on pain pills, endless doctor visits and costly surgeries just to feel good and can instead rely on themselves.

And that really is what each of these reasons comes down to: by building an understanding and unique exercise plan around the way your body moves, we can help you take control of the pain you experience as you age.

Reason #7 - Enhancing the Benefits of Traditional Therapies

When combined with traditional manual therapies, the benefits of movement and strength plans go through the roof. Therapies such as chiropractic, massage, and acupuncture all have a HUGE benefit in helping tissues heal. Each of these therapies improves the function of our joints, muscles, and nervous system in its own unique way and should be included with any movement and strength program.

When we combine the benefits of full-body chiropractic care and manual therapy with full-body movement and strength programs, we can not only help the tissues heal but protect our body from the small irritations that lead to pain. This is what will keep you active and independent without the use of pain pills, endless doctor visits, and costly surgeries.

Reason #8 - A Patient-Centered, Active Approach to Care

In Chapter Two we discussed many of the pitfalls of our current approach to pain management, many of which can be corrected by adding in a movement and strength plan to your treatment plan. It puts the patient at the center of the treatment plan. It keeps us from relying too heavily on passive therapies and helps us benefit from active, movement-based therapies to create results that carry over outside of the clinic.

By focusing on the entire body, a movement and strength plan keeps us from trying to micromanage isolated symptoms. It creates confidence in our daily life and in our body's ability to handle our daily activities and to get rid of that nagging fear that keeps us from doing what we love. Each movement and strength plan can be created with the big picture in mind: creating solutions that help you stay active and strong so you can continue doing the activities you love.

To keep up with our active lifestyles, our body requires us not only to heal, but to protect the body through improved functional strength and better movement patterns.

Combining the benefits of traditional manual therapy with movement and strength programs allows us to properly heal while taking back control of how we feel as we age.

Part Two

In Part One of this book we aimed to provide a better understanding of the flaws in the current approach to pain management and the importance of adding movement and strength training in keeping us active and strong and doing what we love, it's time to get started learning ways to improve the way we move.

In Part Two, our aim is to give you tools to help you move with confidence. These are the exact same tools and cues we use in the clinic to help people overcome pain. By building a better understanding of basic, movement fundamentals we can ensure that we're protecting our bodies outside of the clinic, doing the activities we love. The following chapters will provide practical advice and exercises to improve your movement patterns, functional strength, and mobility so you can move with confidence, overcome pain, and live your life without any limitations.

As you read through Part Two you may start asking yourself, why do I care about the hip hinge, the squat, how to strengthen my hips and shoulders, etc.? Remember: When it comes to non-traumatic injuries, your back pain isn't a back issue.

Your shoulder pain isn't a shoulder issue. They are movement issues. **Which means to SOLVE your issue we have to look at it through a movement lens.**

To answer the question of why should you care; learning these movement patterns, strength principles, and mobility tools holds the key to overcoming your chronic back, knee, shoulder, or hip pain and allowing you to live your life without limitations.

Chapter Five

MOVEMENT PATTERNING 101: BREATHING AND THE HIP HINGE

In Part One of this book we introduced you to the importance of movement and strength training when it comes to avoiding age-related pain and how they will allow you to live your life without limitations. In Part Two we're giving you practical advice that you can use to start moving with confidence. We're going to start off our journey by focusing on ways to improve our movement patterns – how to coordinate movements to perform basic, functional activities.

In this chapter we take a look at two of the most fundamental movement patterns and teach you how to perform them to protect your body from pain and injury.

Breathing and The Diaphragm

The breath is a foundational movement pattern that occurs over 20,000 times a day. It's fascinating when you think about it (at least to us). It's the only movement that we can do voluntarily and involuntarily. Think about it: while breathing happens automatically, we also have the ability to control the rate, depth and frequency of our breath. That is why establishing a proper breathing technique is vital in improving overall movement patterning.

Our diaphragm is the muscle primarily responsible for controlling our breath and breathing mechanics. It separates our chest cavity from our abdomen and has a lot of important structures that pass through it (arteries, veins, muscles, esophagus). By training our breathing mechanics we can not only prevent pain and injury, we can create positive impacts on our digestive, cardiovascular, and musculoskeletal systems.

Breathing and Low Back Pain

Intra-abdominal pressure (IAP) is defined as the pressure within the abdominal cavity. When it comes to low back pain, understanding how to create this pressure is extremely important in creating spinal "stiffness" that protects the spine and reduces the risk of injury.

The best way to envision how IAP creates stiffness to protect the low back is to think of a balloon. In this example your abdominal cavity is the balloon. A fully inflated balloon is stiff and allows little movement when pressed (creating stability). This protects anything inside the balloon (in this example, your spine and intervertebral discs). The less inflated the balloon the less stiffness and the less stability, increasing the risk of injury. We can use this concept in our everyday lives when we go to lift something off the floor.

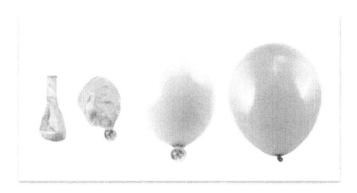

Breathing and Neck Pain

"Chest breathing" is a common breathing mistake we see in the clinic. It's common in people who work long hours at a desk, are dealing with a lot of stress, or are heavy smokers. It's easy to spot when people take a deep breath and their chest rises rather than their abdomen. Instead of utilizing their diaphragm for a full breath they start to use their neck musculature to "lift" the rib cage.

Here's how it works: if the diaphragm isn't doing its job well, muscles in the upper chest (pectoralis minor) and neck (sternocleidomastoid and scalenus) will try to help out with our breathing. These muscles aren't meant to be used this frequently or in this way, causing them to get exhausted and tender. This can lead to neck pain, headaches, and hand numbness/tingling. This is another reason why we always need to start movement training with breathing mechanics.

Breathing and Stress Reduction

The breath is also fascinating as it is the only way we can influence our involuntary (autonomic) nervous system. Things like our heart rate and digestion are controlled by this portion of the nervous system. Slowing down these involuntary processes through breath can both have positive benefits for stress reduction. By slowing down or speeding up our breathing patterns, we have the ability to shift us towards a more parasympathetic (relaxed) state or a more sympathetic (excited) state.

This ability to affect our autonomic nervous system impacts all aspects of our physiology (including cardiovascular and digestive) and is another reason it's important to learn how to control our breath.

How to Properly Perform Diaphragmatic (Belly) Breathing

Belly breathing is an easy exercise to practice:

- Lie on your back with your knees bent and feet flat on the floor

- Place one hand on your belly and the other hand on your chest.

- Take a deep, slow (4-second) inhale through your nose. Your belly should rise before your chest (watch hands). Focus on expanding your belly in all directions (not just pushing your belly out).

- Slowly exhale through the nose while allowing your belly to relax naturally (not sucking in). Pay attention to the stiffness created in your abdomen on the inhale by pressing the abdomen with your finger.

- We obviously can't consciously pay attention to every breath we take, which is why we want this to become automatic. Consistently and repeatedly practicing our breathing technique is the best way to ingrain this pattern and reap the benefits of better breathing.

The Hip Hinge

The hip hinge is THE foundational movement upon which all other movements are built, which is why it's important to spend time creating a better understanding of what the movement should look and feel like. Having a basic understanding of how to bend forward can save you from years of pain. A nice analogy is to compare your low back to a wire hanger. While having the ability to bend, if repeated too often or frequently it will eventually "snap."

A few things to keep in mind as we cover the hip hinge: many people naturally perform a pretty solid hinge. With these people, it's still important to practice and create an understanding of the movement. The first thing to go when people become fatigued is the basic movement patterning. While they may start out with perfect form, as they get tired, they start to lose it. We see it all the time in the gym. By creating a conscious understanding of the hip hinge, we can maintain the proper pattern even as we fatigue and thereby avoid pain and injury that comes from repeated bending of the low back.

The second thing to consider is that it's easy to maintain a proper hip hinge when we're consciously thinking about it. But our goal is to make it automatic. This can only be done through repetition. So even after you understand the hinge, it's important to get the repetitions in. We want to be sure the next time you accidentally drop something (or perform another unexpected movement) you automatically default to a good, strong spine position rather than an unstable rounding of the low back.

Defining the Term "Neutral Spine"

Throughout the rest of this book you'll notice me throwing out the term "neutral spine," so it's important to have an idea of what I mean by it. Neutral spine is the natural position of the spine when all three curves are present and in good alignment. It is the strongest position of the spine and ensures that movements of our daily life are being distributed correctly to help avoid early wear and tear.

How to Perform the Hip Hinge

To perform a proper hip hinge there are two main things to pay attention to:

1. **Maintaining Neutral Spine**

   As we move through the movement it's important to maintain a strong spinal position. A good way to determine if you're in neutral spine is to place a PVC pipe or other long, skinny object (such as a broom or mop handle) along your spine. The pipe should be touching three points: the back of your head, your mid-back, and your pelvis. There will be a natural curve in the low back and neck that will not be touching the pipe. As you perform the hip hinge, it's important all three points maintain contact with the pipe and the natural curves are maintained.

2. **Initiate the Movement by Sending the Hips Back**

When bending forward it is imperative that we initiate the movement by reaching our hips back. This keeps the movement in the hips and our center of gravity over our weight-bearing joints.

Image: Dr. Baird demonstrating the proper three-point contact hinge technique

The Five Most Common Hip Hinge Mistakes

Now that we know what "normal" looks like, let's look at five of the most common mistakes we see in the clinic that can lead to pain and injury and should therefore be avoided:

1. **Rounding in the Back**

   This is the most common of the mistakes and usually the easiest to spot. Rounding of the back creates too much spinal flexion and is the number one contributor to non-traumatic low back pain. With a PVC, this is seen when the pole comes off the pelvis as shown in the first picture below.

2. **Not Sending Hips Back**

   In this mistake, the patient hinges at the hips and can keep a neutral spine but fails to send their hips back. This puts their center of gravity too far forward and will easily lead to low back rounding/pain. This can be seen when neutral spine is maintained but legs remain straight (no bend in knee), as shown in the second picture below.

3. **The "Hinge Squat" (too much knee bend)**

   While sending your hips back will create a small amount of knee flexion, the only "movement" should be at the hips. With too much knee bend we lose the tension in our hamstrings that is imperative in lifting and other activities that require us to generate power from the hips. This mistake is demonstrated in the third picture below.

4. Extension in the Thoracic Spine

   A mistake usually seen in the hypermobile individual is overextension in the thoracic spine. This mistake is demonstrated in the fourth picture below. It's hard to see in this picture (because I'm the opposite of hypermobile), but what you'll see with these patients is the thoracic spine coming off the PVC while maintaining contact with the back of head and the pelvis.

5. Rocking the Pelvis Forward

   A lot of patients will hyper-extend their low back while initiating their hip hinge. This can lead to mistake number four (extension in thoracic spine) or dumping the pelvis forward, putting more pressure on the lumbar facet joints and contributing to pain.

This is also subtler but is seen as patients initiate the squat. Look for the pelvis to move before they send their hips back.

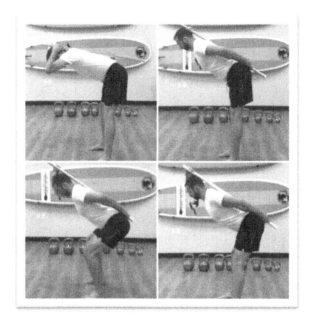

Most common hip hinge mistakes: Rounding the low back (top left), not sending hips back (top right), the "hinge-squat" (bottom left), overextension of the mid back (bottom right).

The Breath and Hinge while Sitting

Many of our clients have jobs that require long hours of sitting. Maintaining a good spinal position during this time is essential for remaining pain free. Sitting often leads to rounding forward of the shoulders and head as well as the middle and lower back. The good news is that the same principles of breath and hinging can be applied to the sitting position as well. While sitting in your chair sit up tall and find your neutral spine. If you need to lean forward, maintain your neutral spine and keep all the movements in your hip.

The Top 10 Hip Hinge Progressions

In order to train the hip hinge safely and effectively, we'll often need to progress or regress the hip hinge to suit a client's ability level. The following are 10 progressions that train and ingrain the hip hinge in unique ways. (A reminder that videos of all these exercises can be found on the Evolve Performance Healthcare YouTube Channel.)

1. **Hero Squats**

   Hero squats are a good place to start with those who are having trouble keeping movement at the hips and/or unlocking at the hips to initiate the movement. By taking the knees out of the equation, patients are forced to hinge at the hips.

2. **Butt Taps**

   Progressing to a standing position, butt taps are good for those who need work on unlocking at the hips. Having the wall as a cue and "reaching" back with your hips is a great way to teach clients how to keep their center of gravity over their weight-bearing joints.

3. **Three-Point Contact Hinge**

   Once the concept of unlocking at the hips is mastered, we need to focus on keeping a neutral spine. This is best introduced with the three-point contact hip hinge. Keeping the PVC on the back of the head, thoracic spine, and pelvis is a nice cue to keep the spine neutral when going through the movement.

4. **Banded Hip Hinge**

   Now that unlocking at the hips and neutral spine can be maintained, it's time to further engrain the pattern by adding resistance. The banded hip hinge is an easy way to add resistance to the hip hinge pattern.

5. **Weighted Hip Hinge**

   Incorporate heavier weights and begin transition to more functional movements (lifting) with the weighted hip hinge. This is also a great hamstring mobilization tool!

6. **KB Lift**

   Now that we've learned to hinge and recognize how to build tension in the hamstrings, we can use that tension to safely lift weight up off the floor. The Kettlebell lift is a great way to train proper lifting technique.

7. **Hinge to Squat**

   The hinge easily lends itself to other functional movements, including the squat. The Hinge to Squat teaches the body how to transition the hip hinge to the squat movement.

8. **Banded Pull Through**

   With the hip hinge mastered, it's now time to learn how to use the hinge to generate power from the hips for more athletic activities. Banded pull throughs are a great way to safely train the hip thrust.

9. **KB Swing**

   When done correctly, kettlebell swings help further engrain the hip hinge pattern while also teaching our bodies how to generate power from the hips. Lifting the weight involves shooting the hips forward (using the momentum to lift weight) while "catching" the weight should be done in a perfect hinge position.

10. Clean

The most advanced movement will likely take months to years to master. The clean uses the hip hinge, lift, hip thrust, and full squat to accomplish — demonstrating a clear understanding of movement patterns and full-body mobility/stability. Keep in mind that professional athletes spend years of their life mastering this movement, which is very hard to perfect.

Conclusion

While seemingly simple movements, the breath and the hip hinge are two of the most important movements to master. Understanding and mastering these two movements can save you from years of back and neck pain, headaches, and other ailments that keep you from doing the things you love. Remember: our goal isn't to just understand these movements and move on but to make them automatic. We want them to become our default movement patterns so we perform them without having to consciously think about them. This is only achieved through repetition. Get those repetitions in!

Chapter Six

Now that we've got a better handle on two of the foundational movement patterns, the breath and the hinge, we're ready to progress to more functional movement patterns. The lift, squat, and lunge are three of the most important movement patterns that we use on a DAILY basis and are important to train to protect our bodies from pain and injury.

The Lift

The next progression from the hinge is how to use the hinge to lift weight off the floor. This is obviously important in the fitness world and is also used through our daily lives.

To perform the lift there are two main cues to pay attention to:

1. **Maintain Neutral Spine**
   Just like with the hinge, maintaining a strong spinal position is the most important factor in preventing pain and injury during the lift. Most injuries with the lift are the result of rounding the back prior to (or while) lifting a heavy weight.

2. **Develop Tension in the Hamstrings**
   The lift is designed to strengthen our prime movers (the glutes and hamstrings). It is NOT meant to be a low back exercise.

Before we lift any weight off the ground, we must first raise our hips (while maintaining a neutral spine) to develop tension in the hamstrings/glutes. We then use this tension to lift the weight. We should NEVER feel any strain in the low back.

Image: Dr. Baird Demonstrating the Proper Lifting Technique

The Squat

The squat is a foundational movement that demonstrates proper movement patterning along with adequate mobility and stability of the entire body. It's used a lot in the fitness world but is also important in most activities we perform.

To perform the squat there are three main cues to pay attention to:

1. **Unlock at the Hips**

    We need to begin our descent into the squat by unlocking at the hips. This ensures we keep weight over our weight-bearing joints while engaging our posterior chain of muscles.

2. **Maintain Neutral Spine**

    Just like the hinge and lift, maintaining a strong spinal position is the most important factor in preventing pain and injury with the squat.

3. **Stance**

    How far apart should your feet be? Should the toes be pointed forward? The answer? It depends. Each person has a unique shape to their pelvis and hip socket that will determine their ideal stance. The width of your stance should be determined by allowing you the furthest descent while maintaining a neutral spine.

The Three Most Common Squat Mistakes

Now that we know what normal looks like, let's look at three of the most common mistakes we see in the clinic:

1. **Unlocking at the Knees**

    When descending into the squat, many people (especially those who are on the more mobile side) will start the descent by unlocking at the knees. This will put a lot of force through the knee which will eventually lead to pain. When squatting

UNLOCKING AT THE HIPS is the most important cue to remember.

2. **Squatting Too Low**

    The unarguable requisite to safe and effective squat patterning is the maintenance of a neutral spine throughout the full range of motion. A common mistake people make when performing the squat is going lower than their body is able. This creates a compensation that has been termed the "butt wink". The butt wink is a backward rotation of the pelvis that causes a rounding of the lumbar spine. This is an unstable position for the spine and can cause serious injury (especially when heavy weights are added!).

3. **Narrow Stance**

    Most people, at some point in their lives, were told that proper squat positioning means their feet are hip distance apart with their toes pointed forward. The problem with this theory is that every body (especially the hips and pelvis) is shaped just a little bit differently. If our stance is too narrow for our body shape, it can cause our chest to fall forward or pinch in the front of the hips.

Squat Variations and Their Clinical Significance

If you've ever taken a boot camp class or watched people in the gym you probably know there are a lot of variations of the squat. Ever wonder what the difference was? Each variation of the squat loads the body differently and can have a unique benefit when used clinically. Here's a break-down of seven of the most common squat variations, and we'll discuss how each can be used in a clinical or rehabilitation setting.

1. **Back Squat**

    The back squat is performed by placing the resistance on our upper shoulders (behind the head).

    Clinical Significance: Strengthens lower extremity posterior chain and so is great for hamstring, hip, and low back rehabilitation. Good indicator of hip and ankle mobility. Demonstrates movement overall quality (ability to hip hinge, keep trunk upright, etc.)

2. **Front Squat**

    The front squat is performed by holding the resistance in front of our body with elbows pointed forward.

    Clinical Significance: Places a stronger emphasis on the quadriceps muscle making it great for knee rehabilitation. It is also a good indicator of hip and ankle mobility while also demonstrating any deficiencies in shoulder/elbow/wrist mobility.

3. **Sumo Squat**

    Performed with a wide stance with toes pointed outward (generally a 45-degree angle).

    Clinical Significance: The sumo squat requires greater hip mobility and places a stronger emphasis on the adductor (groin) muscle group. Great for improving hip mobility and rehabbing groin strains.

4. **Bulgarian Split Squat**

    Performed in a split stance with rear leg elevated on a bench (or chair, etc.). Resistance can be added by holding dumbbells, kettlebell, or placing weight on the upper back/shoulders.

    Clinical Significance: Unilateral movement allows for training of side-to-side imbalances. Incorporates a balance challenge. Strengthens the quadriceps muscle for improved knee stability.

5. **Goblet Squat**

    Similar to a front squat but performed holding a kettlebell or dumbbell (in front of body).

    Clinical Significance: Similar to front squat, lighter weight allows you to sit in squat position and work on hip/ankle mobility. Weight distribution often allows for greater squat depth.

6. **Pistol Squat**

    Also called a single leg squat. The pistol squat is performed by squatting with one leg, while the other leg and arms are flexed forward to provide counter-balance.

    Clinical Significance: Improves hip and ankle mobility. Unilateral stance allows correcting side to side imbalances and furthers balance challenge.

7. **Overhead Squat**

    Full squat performed while holding weight overhead.

    Clinical Significance: Demonstrates mobility/stability of the entire body. Increases demands for shoulder stability and core strength. Improves overall movement quality.

The Lunge

The lunge is one of the most functional exercises — meaning that it most readily translates to real-world activities. Walking, running, hiking, and jumping all require the same muscle groups that we train with lunges.

Pain Free Lunging

Forward Lunge

Anterior knee pain is very common for people who do a lot of forward lunges. The reason is that the forward lunge is a "quad dominant" exercise, which relies heavily on the eccentric contraction of the quadricep muscle to control the movement. This puts a huge amount of load through the knee-cap and patellar tendon.

Here's the truth: if you crank out forward lunges for long enough, they will catch up to you. It doesn't matter how perfect your form is; the repeated pull on the knee-cap and patellar tendon will lead to discomfort, pain, and injury.

Reverse Lunge

With that said, a safer version of the lunge is the reverse lunge. While seemingly similar, they are NOT the same. A few key differences:

- By stepping back, our forward leg is in a CLOSED chain, meaning it remains on the floor. This allows for more control and stability in our entire leg.
- It is posterior chain dominant, meaning we're loading our hamstrings and glutes vs. putting too much tension through our

quads and the patellar tendon (which is heavily stressed in the forward lunge).

Lunges are one of the most functional exercises for translating to real-world activities and should be part of any lower body strength and movement program to stay pain free. Knowing the difference between the two types of lunges and how to properly progress the lunge, we can continue to build strength while keeping our body safe from injury!

Building Strength and Coordination with Different Lunge Progressions

Exercise progressions and regressions are important and often underutilized in the clinical and fitness setting. Being able to change the difficulty of the exercise to fit a client ability level ensures we build confidence in our body's ability to perform the way we want and helps avoid plateaus in our rehabilitation and performance goals.

The lunge is a great exercise to progress as a way to further ingrain movement patterns, build strength, and mobilize our hips and ankles. Let's look at some common lunge progressions that we use in the clinic. (And remember that videos of all these exercises can be found on the Evolve Performance Healthcare YouTube channel.)

1. **Static Lunges**

   Starting in a lunge position (feet spread and staggered), drop back knee to the ground and raise back up.

2. **Step Up**

   Starting with a 12" box or stool, simply step up. This can be easily progressed by holding weights in each hand or raising opposite knee (to add a balance challenge).

3. **Forward Lunge**

   From a standing position step your right foot forward into a full lunge position. Left knee should touch the ground before pressing off your right foot and return to standing position. Right knee should not go over right toe.

4. **Reverse Lunge**

   From a standing position step your right foot backward into a full lunge position, knee touching floor. Press off your front foot to return to standing position. Front knee should not go over right toe. Knee can touch the ground but should not be resting.

5. **Reverse Lunge Slide**

   Place one foot on a fitness slider (or paper towel on hard surface) and slide foot backward. Press off front foot to return to starting position.

6. **Lateral Lunge**

   Lunge progression into a new plane of movement (coronal plane). From a standing position step your right foot to the left into a full side lunge position. Return to starting position and repeat.

7. **Star Lunges**

   Integrating lunge patterns into different planes of movement. From a standing position, step your right foot into a full forward lunge position. Return to starting position and immediately perform side lunge. Return to starting position and immediately perform backward lunge.

8. **Forward Lunge into Reverse Lunge**

    An advanced lunge progression. From a standing position, step your right foot forward into a full lunge position. Press off your front foot and immediately move into a reverse lunge. Repeat for one minute on each side. This one should burn!

9. **Weighted Reverse Lunges**

    One of the best ways to build function strength in our legs. Holding dumbbells in each hand, perform a reverse lunge, holding weights on each side of the front leg.

10. **Bowler Lunge**

    Starting on left foot, bring right foot back and reach to the left, tapping the right toe on ground and return to the starting position (imagine the ending position of a professional bowler).

Conclusion

We hope you're starting to see how improving basic, fundamental movement principles can have a huge impact on your ability to do what you love. Not only does improving movement patterns protect our joints from the repeated irritations that lead to pain and injury, but each movement can be progressed to improve functional strength and mobility to help build confidence in our body's ability to do what we love.

With a solid foundation of what movement should look (and feel like) we can begin our discussion on building strength.

In the next few chapters we'll focus on ways to improve strength of the entire body to ensure our bodies are able to handle the tasks of our daily life.

Chapter Seven

Going all the way back to Chapter 1 we discussed the three things to focus on to improve overall movement: patterning, functional strength, and mobility. In Chapters 5 and 6 we covered how to improve movement patterning (breath, hinge, lift, squat, lunge) to better coordinate movements and protect our joints during functional activities. In the next two chapters we'll discuss how to improve functional strength to protect our joints and make sure our bodies are strong enough to adequately handle the activities that we love to do! We start with the spine, the foot and the core.

A Quick Note About Functional Strength

Before we begin, we want to clarify what we mean by "functional strength." When we use this term, we mean building the strength required to perform the activities in your daily life. It's 100% unique to the individual and depends on what you do. If you have to sit a lot at work, functional strength would entail building the muscles that will keep you upright and able to resist the gravitation forces that pull you down. If you're a construction worker, functional strength entails being able to lift, carry, and spend all day on your feet. We need you to be able to perform those activities without hurting yourself.

Functional strength is different than traditional training, where goals are usually more aesthetic (lose weight, build six-pack abs, or get huge chests and biceps). Functional strength is about making sure your body is strong enough to handle the activities of your life so you can live your life without any limitations. OK...now let's get started!

The Spine

Spinal Stabilization

"A stable and well-organized spine is the key to moving safely and effectively and maximizing power output and force production." - Kelly Starrett, *Becoming a Supple Leopard*

Our spine protects the most important part of our body (the central nervous system), which is the reason it's so important we protect it all costs. Any injury to our spine or spinal cord will have life altering consequences. A disorganized spine will also lead to compensation patterns that impact our hips, shoulders, knees, and feet. We HAVE to bring awareness to how we stabilize our spine or we will automatically revert to faulty movement patterns that set us up for injury.

Learning to brace our spine properly is the number-one most important concept to master before beginning any movement routine and a great way to protect our spine throughout our day.

How to Brace Your Spine Properly

Remember from a previous discussion that our muscles should be doing most of the stabilizing of the body. Any time our muscles are weak or fail to engage, we rely on our passive stabilizers (ligaments, bones, discs) for stabilization and this is where most injuries occur. Knowing the importance of spinal bracing, here is how we can easily do it:

- Squeeze you butt as hard as you can (set your pelvis)
- Pull your rib cage down
- Get your belly tight
- Set your head to neutral and screw in your shoulders

Are You in a Good Spinal Position?

The "Two Hand Rule" is a great way to check in to see if our ribcage and pelvis are set in a neutral and strong position. To perform is easy:

- Place one thumb on sternum – palm down
- Place other thumb on pubic bone – palm down

The goal is to keep the hands in parallel planes. Someone who is rounded too far forward will notice their hands coming closer together while those with an overextended low back and flared ribcage will see their two hands moving farther apart. We will also lose proper positioning if our pelvis is rotated forward or backward. This exercise can be performed standing, sitting, or lying down.

Are You Braced?

We obviously can't maintain full spinal bracing as we go about our day but it is important to maintain a certain level of bracing throughout the day to protect our spine through our daily activities. The "Belly Whack Test" is a way to help bring consciousness to our braced position concept. It's a pretty simple idea in that we should always be walking around with about 20% tension so that we could take a "whack" to the belly. If you've got a spongy middle, you'll get caught — which means your spine is at a higher risk for injury.

The Foot

Foot Strength – The Basics

Our foot is the foundation for all movement. Any movement we make begins with the foot's ability to absorb and transfer those forces up the kinetic chain. A weak foot struggles to absorb these forces and is the reason it's one of the most common contributors to knee, hip, and low back pain. Our culture's strong reliance on cushioned shoes along with artificial support (orthotics) has led to weak feet that are unprepared to absorb the impact forces of running. This contributes to knee, hip, and low back pain and easily gets exacerbated with any increase in mileage we make in our active lifestyles.

In order to better absorb ground reactive forces, it's important to strengthen the small intrinsic muscles of the foot. Due to the heavy cushioned and supportive shoes we regularly wear, these muscles often don't have to work hard — leading to foot weakness. This is part of the reason you've probably noticed a strong trend toward more barefoot/minimalist shoes. The following three exercises will help regain functional strength of your foot:

1. Toe Yoga

   Toe yoga provides improved control of foot movement while strengthening intrinsic muscle of the foot.

   How to Perform: With foot flat on ground, raise big toe (keeping other four toes on ground). Next, raise other four toes (leaving big toe on ground). Last, splay all five toes apart. Note: Cramping may occur as these small muscles are not used to working.

2. Toe Presses

   Toe presses further strengthen the small, intrinsic muscles of our foot while also supporting our arch.

   How to Perform: With feet flat on the floor, press toes into the floor while attempting to lift arch off of floor. Hold for 5 seconds, release, and repeat. Note: This is an isometric contraction (meaning there shouldn't be any movement).

3. Toe Leans

   Toe leans are a full-body strengthening exercise that supports the foot in a more functional way.

   How to perform: Stand facing a wall (about two feet away). Keep your body in a straight line and slowly lean forward. The goal is to find the angle that you can hold (using your feet) without falling all the way forward. When you get past the point you can hold, let yourself fall and catch your body on the wall with your hands, reset, and repeat.

These three exercises are extremely beneficial at strengthening the small, intrinsic muscles of the foot. In addition, we strongly recommend spending more time barefoot – whether that's just walking around the house or in your training routine (as long as it's safe and pain free, of course!)

Foot Mobility

As the foundation for most movements, the foot will dictate how much force gets transferred up the kinetic chain to the knees, hips, and low back. Just as important as improving foot strength, improving foot mobility is equally as essential. A general rule of thumb when it comes to foot health is:

A STIFF FOOT = LESS SHOCK ABSORPTION = MORE FORCE TRANSFERRED UP THE BODY = MORE PAIN AND INJURY

A MORE MOBILE AND STRONG FOOT = BETTER SHOCK ABSORPTION = LESS FORCE TRANSFERRED UP THE BODY = LESS PAIN AND INJURY

With the idea that a mobile and strong foot is better able to protect us from injury, let's take a look at some of the common areas of stiffness in the foot/ankle.

Where to Improve Foot Mobility

1. Ankle

    One of the most common missing ranges of motion that we see leading to poor shock absorption is ankle dorsiflexion. A normal ankle should have around 45 degrees of ankle dorsiflexion when planted on the floor. Missing ankle dorsiflexion decreases the foots ability to absorb ground reactive forces and leads to increase strain up the kinetic chain. It also causes other movement compensations that lead to a variety of other injuries

2. **Big Toe**

    Another common area where range of motion is missing and can lead to big problems up the kinetic chain is the big toe. Adequate range of motion (around 65 degrees) is needed to avoid compensations that place strains anywhere up the kinetic chain (arch of foot, knee, hips, etc.). The foot is one of the most overlooked areas of the body. Limitations in strength and mobility can be seen anywhere up the kinetic chain, which is why building a strong and mobile foot is one of the most important things to address when aiming to keep active and live our life without limitations.

Why You Don't Need Orthotics

Orthotics present one of the most commonly asked questions in the clinic when it comes to treating foot and knee pain. You've probably even been prescribed orthotics at some point in your life to treat foot, ankle, knee, or even hip pain.

The biggest myth in the manual therapy world is that orthotics "fix" foot, knee and hip pain. While they provide short-term relief allowing you to live with a problem, they always fail to provide the long-term solutions that will keep you active – regardless of what shoes you're wearing.

Orthotics are most commonly prescribed because you have foot, knee, or hip pain and the doctor decided that a lack of support in your foot is the cause. They contour to your foot and provide an artificial arch to provide a passive support of the foot. <u>By providing only passive support, orthotics fail to correct the underlying problem</u>. The alignment and strength issues of the feet that lead to foot, ankle, knee and hip pain are still there and will continue to contribute to your pain.

Orthotics are a crutch, allowing you to live with a problem without actually correcting it. They provide support so your muscles, joints, and ligaments don't have to. Is that really the solution you want? What happens when you don't wear your orthotics? Guess what? The pain comes back.

How to Achieve Foot Support Without Relying on Orthotics

For long-term, sustainable results that carry over into your active lifestyle, here are a few things you could be doing instead of using orthotics:

1. **Correct Toes**
   Instead of orthotics, we prescribe Correct Toes: a natural way to restore proper alignment of our feet and begin building proper support for our feet.

2. **Strengthen the Intrinsic Muscles of Your Foot**
   Our body should have the ability to support itself without the use of passive supports. As we're wearing shoes all day, the shoes do provide most of the support, so the small intrinsic

muscles of the foot don't have to work — becoming weak and contributing to pain.

3. **Lower Extremity Strength Programming**

   Building strength, control, and coordination of the entire low extremity helps control how we load our feet and prevents over-pronation, which heavily contributes to foot and knee pain.

Choosing the Right Shoe for Foot Health

The amount of pain we experience when running can almost always be traced back to the shoes we wear. Our culture's strong reliance on cushioned shoes along with artificial support (orthotics) has led to weak feet that are unprepared to absorb the impact forces of running. This contributes to knee, hip, and low back pain and easily gets exacerbated with the many miles put in to reach our running goals.

When it comes to picking the right shoe for you, we should trade in the highly cushioned or stiff shoes for shoes that encourage proper alignment, strength, and movement of our feet. Here are the things you should be looking for when picking your next shoe:

- Widest in the toe box (better alignment)
- No heel elevation (better strength)
- Flexible soles (better movement)

Transitioning to the Right Shoe

It's also important to note that it's not a smart idea to go straight from a highly cushioned and/or supported shoe straight to a highly flexible and minimalist shoe. The joints and tissues need time to adapt to the new alignment and movement in the foot. Finding the right transition shoes can help your feet (and body) adapt to the more natural footwear.

The Core

What Is Our Core?

For most in the fitness world, the word "core" has been used interchangeably with the word "abs". A core workout has meant an ab workout. In reality, our core includes every muscle that attaches to our pelvis (47 total, spanning the entire body). And for that reason, core strengthening programs require us to integrate and coordinate full-body, functional movements.

Part of the recent popularity of Olympic lifting in the fitness and therapy world (squats, deadlifts, cleans, etc.) is that these movements strengthen the core through improving strength, power, and coordination of the entire body.

Core Strength vs. Core Coordination

Traditionally when individuals talk about core training, they are talking about core strength. How long can you hold a plank? How many sit-ups can you do? When it comes to injury prevention and recovery it's vital to differentiate core strength and core coordination, because they are not the same thing.

Research has shown that core stabilization relies more on "proprioception and timing rather than gross muscular strength" (Gray Cook). In other words, core stability requires more coordination (proper firing of muscles) rather than isolated strength. Injuries happen when the key muscles that protect our spine don't fire correctly. A simple truth is:

Most people don't get hurt from a lack of core strength. Most people get hurt from a lack of core coordination.

Think about it: most low back injuries happen when we're doing something rather innocuous (bending over to pick something up, pulling up our pants, reaching to catch something that we drop). It's not that our muscles aren't strong enough to lift our pants up (at least I hope not); it's that the muscle didn't activate when we needed it to and all the force went through our spine.

How to Improve Core Coordination

Improving core coordination requires a different approach than training core strength.

1. **Training Rotation Patterns**
    While the science and anatomy regarding the benefit of rolling patterns could have a book of its own, suffice it to say that rolling patterns require us to recruit and coordinate the firing of deeper core musculature. An ability to start and stop movement at the core prevents forces from being transferred through our spine.

2. **Proprioception/Balance Training**
    Gray Cook, a leader in movement science and thinking, describes core stabilization as being proprioceptively driven. An

improved ability to know where our body is in space will increase the proper firing of muscles to protect our spine and extremity joints. Something as simple as adding a balance pad or BOSU ball to your workout can aid in improving core coordination.

3. **Full-Body Movements**

    In daily life, our muscles don't operate independently. Strengthening isolated "core" musculature through sit-ups, toes-to-bars, etc. fails to protect us in real-life situations. Full-body core exercises require the integration of all muscles of the core to improve firing patterns when it matters most. Exercises like the farmers carry are an excellent core coordination exercise that require proper coordination of the entire body.

Protecting Our Spine with Core Strength

Developing core strength shouldn't be about building a six pack. Instead, a strong core is one that has the ability to absorb the forces of our daily activities and prevent them from going through our more passive stabilizers (the spine, discs, ligaments, etc.). To do this we need our cores to be better prepared to limit or stop movement, rather than the traditional exercises that initiate movement.

There are hundreds of exercises that strengthen and train the core. The majority of these exercises "initiate" movement. Sit-ups, toes-to-bars, hollow rocks, stir-the-pots, and mountain climbers all utilize our core muscles to initiate a movement. In the therapeutic fitness world, we're seeing a huge shift towards the importance of using core exercises to stop unwanted or unnecessary movement. Using core movements that stop movement rather than initiate movement requires more control and improves the proper timing and firing of deeper core musculature for greater strength and stability.

The Suitcase Carry and Pallof Press are good examples of this. With the Suitcase Carry we carry a heavy weight in one hand. This requires us to use our core stabilizers to prevent our bodies from crumbling to the side. With the Pallof Press we hold a band in front of our chest that is hooked to a pole to the side of us, utilizing our core to prevent the band from pulling us to the side. (Both exercises can be found on our YouTube page.)

How to SAFELY Improve Core Strength

You can go on YouTube and find hundreds to thousands of ways to "creatively" (a nice way to put it) strengthen your core. The problem is that the majority of these exercises are unsafe and will lead to pain and injury if performed repeatedly. When it comes to strengthening our core there is beauty in simplicity. Planks, anti-movement, and crawls are categories of exercises that SAFELY strengthen our core and can easily be progressed and regressed to fit your current ability level.

1. Planks

    A staple in core strengthening, the traditional plank exercise offers a variety of progressions to challenge the superficial and deeper muscles of the core in a variety of planes of motion.

2. Anti-Movement Exercise

Discussed in the previous section, exercises that train our core to limit movement provide a powerful and safe way to functionally strengthen the core. Examples include the Farmer's Carry and Pallof Press (find videos on our YouTube channel).

3. Crawling

Crawling turns traditional core strengthening into a full body exercise that requires strength, control, and movement coordination. These moves mimic activities we perform in the real world and are important for building functional strength.

Building a solid foundation for strength is imperative before we progress to exercises with heavier weight or more complex movement patterns. Learning how to properly brace the spine, improve how we absorb ground reactive forces (through strong and mobile feet), and strengthen our core through full-body, coordinated movements sets the foundation to build the strength of our stronger muscle groups, which we discuss in the next chapter.

Chapter Eight

With a solid foundation of spine, foot and core strength we can now shift focus to building functional strength in our hips and shoulders. Depending on your daily activities, these two areas are cornerstones to preventing pain and dysfunction in the entire body. In this chapter, we discuss how deficiencies in hip and shoulder strength can lead to injury and provide solutions about how to protect your body so you can live life without limitations.

The Hips

"Our glutes are the cornerstone of hip and pelvic stability and creating a bulletproof body that fends off the likelihood of chronic lower back pain and dysfunction." - Dr. John Rusin

Protecting Your Low Back with Hip Strength

What's the strongest and arguably the most important muscle in the body? Your glute max (your butt). Lying at the transition between our upper and lower extremity the glute max is vitally important in stabilizing our pelvis and spine, developing power in more athletic movements, and controlling the movement of our lower extremity in walking, running, lunging — really ANYTHING.

Guess what muscles we don't use when we sit on our butts all day? You guessed it...our glute max. When the glutes are weak, the hamstrings and lumbar erector muscles compensate by taking up more of the work and therefore are placed under greater stress. Pain often presents in the hamstring or low back (even when glute weakness is the cause). The hip flexors become overactive, and when this happens, there is marked anterior tilt of the pelvis and a lordotic curve at the lumbar spine.

Any program to improve full-body strength needs to include programming to strengthen our glute max!

Protecting Your Feet and Knees with Hip Strength

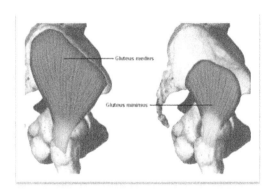

Our glute area (butt area) is a complex of three muscle groups that all help protect our bodies in unique and important ways. Our glute medius and minimus muscles are located on the lateral side of our hips and control hip and leg movement in the coronal (side to side) plane. Deficiencies in glute med and min strength cause our leg to hyper-abduct, or cross the body when we run and walk. This lack of strength in the glute medius and minimus causes a number of problems for active individuals, including:

- Over-pronation of the foot (leading to plantar fasciosis and shin splints);

- Increased strain on the lateral knee (IT band) from a higher valgus force; and

- Higher impact at the knee, hip and low back.

- By strengthening our glute med and min we can maintain better control of where our foot lands when we walk, run, jump, (anything!) and prevent foot, knee, and hip pain.

Most Common Cause of Back Pain in Desk Workers

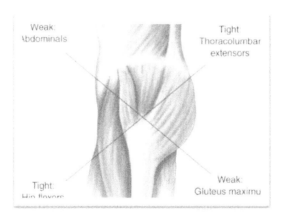

Lower Cross Syndrome is one of the most common deficiencies we see in active individuals who sit long periods for work. It is characterized by a "cross" pattern of weak and overactive muscles. The typical pattern is weakness of the glute max combined with weakness in the lower abdominals and tightness in our hip flexors and hamstrings as they are forced to work harder to compensate for these weaknesses. This leads to a host of issues, including a forward rounding of the pelvis and over-extension of the lower spine. This places increased stress on the lower back and eventually leads to pain and discomfort. Another example of where you may be experiencing back pain or hamstring tightness – but the problem is weak hips!

The Safest and Most Effective Ways to Strengthen Your Glute Complex

Training the glutes does not need to be overly complicated. You do not need hundreds of different exercises to strengthen your hips effectively. Variations and progressions of simple movement patterns are all you need to guarantee you engage and strengthen your glutes to eliminate back pain and keep up your active lifestyle. Bridging, lifting, lunging, and squatting are categories of exercises that SAFELY strengthen your hips and can easily be progressed and regressed to fit your current ability level.

1. Bridging

    Glute bridges are the easiest and safest way to safely introduce glute strengthening into your routine. The can easily be progressed to more difficult variations to meet your particular strength goals.

    How to Perform: Lie on your back with your knees bent and feet flat on the floor. Bring your heels as close to your hips as possible, engage your core, and press through your heels to lift your hips from the ground. Work should be felt in your glutes (butt) area. If you are feeling it in the hamstrings it may mean your feet are too far away from your hips and you should try to bring them in closer.

2. **Lifting**

   Adding weight to the movement patterns discussed in Chapter 6 is the best way to further ingrain those movement patterns while building functional strength. Lifting weight from the floor is one of the most functional and easiest ways to strengthen our entire posterior chain (glutes, hamstrings, low back, etc.).

3. **Squatting**

   Discussed in Chapter 6, squatting is a full body movement that ingrains movement patterns, improves mobility and can easily be progressed with weights to strengthen our glute and hamstring complex. Once we've mastered the squat movement patterns, we can simply add resistance to further challenge our glute/hamstring complex.

4. **Lunging**

   Also discussed in Chapter 6, lunging (in particular reverse lunges) provide a safe way to strengthen our glute complex in a functional way that translates to many of the activities we perform in our daily life. As with the squat, once we can perform a reverse lunge with proper control and balance, we can begin to build strength by simply adding weight.

As you can see, building strength is often as simple as progressing from the movement patterns we discussed in previous chapters. It's also the reason it's so important to ingrain those movement patterns first before we start trying to add a lot of weight. We get hurt when we try to add weight or resistance before we've mastered the basic movement patterns.

Remember our motto: "Move Well. Then Move Often."

The Shoulder

The shoulder is found at the transition between our neck, back and arm, and building shoulder strength is important in treating and preventing all neck, back, and shoulder pain. Due to the anatomy of the shoulder, building strength is slightly more complicated and detailed than the hip. In this chapter we discuss the basic anatomy, common issues that lead to neck, back and shoulder pain and easy ways to begin strengthening our shoulder complex.

Quick note: If you're currently dealing with shoulder pain, a more thorough look and specific plan will be required that goes beyond the purpose of this book.

Shoulder Anatomy

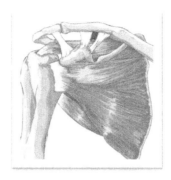

While often described as a "ball and socket" joint, the anatomy of the shoulder is better described as a golf ball sitting on a golf tee: the "ball" is much larger than the "socket." This means the shoulder requires a lot more help from the muscles surrounding the joint (the rotator cuff) to provide stability and control, which makes it more susceptible to injury.

The Shoulder Complex

When it comes to overcoming pain and improving shoulder function, it's important to view the shoulder joint as more of a "complex" that involves the shoulder joint, the thoracic spine, and the shoulder blade. All three work together to ensure the proper coordination of movement to keep our shoulders strong and healthy.

1. The Shoulder Joint

    The shoulder joint itself includes the head of the humerus (our upper arm bone) and where it meets with the glenoid fossa of the shoulder blade. It is held in place by the muscles of the rotator cuff.

2. **The Thoracic Spine**

    The shoulder is inherently connected to your thoracic spine (mid back). Any limitations in the mobility of the mid back will lead to a loss of range of motion in the shoulder and contribute to any shoulder pain you may be experiencing.

3. **The Scapula (Shoulder Blade)**

    The third aspect of the shoulder complex is the shoulder blade itself. With muscular connections that span the entire body, gaining proper movement and control of the shoulder blade is a vital piece of creating strong and healthy shoulders.

We can't improve the function of our shoulder without improving all three portions of the complex.

Improving Shoulder Health for Upper Cross Syndrome

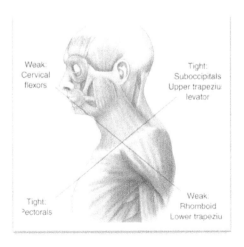

Similar to Lower Cross Syndrome, which we see at the hips, Upper Cross Syndrome is one of the most common deficiencies we see in active individuals who sit for long periods at work. It usually presents as pain in the mid back or anterior shoulder. The classic signs include forward head carriage and overly rounded mid back.

Upper Cross Syndrome is characterized by a "cross" pattern of weak and overactive muscles. The typical pattern is weakness of the lower trapezius combined with weakness in our deeper neck stabilizers and tightness in our pec muscles and upper traps as they are forced to work harder to compensate for these weaknesses. This leads to a host of issues including a rounding forward of the shoulders and drawing forward of the head. These imbalances place extra stress on the neck, back and shoulder, commonly carrying over into the real world by leading to further pain and dysfunction.

How to Strengthen the Shoulder for Less Pain and Improved Function

Similar to the hip, the simplest exercises are the most effective at strengthening the shoulder. Building strength for pain-free shoulders requires us to stop training the individual muscles and start training full-body, functional movements. In the shoulder those movements include **the push, the pull, and the press.**

1. The Push

    Push exercises involve pushing weight away from us and generally work our pectoral muscles and other shoulder muscles on the front of the body. Examples include bench press, push-ups, pec flys, etc.

2. **The Pull**

    Strengthening the back side of our shoulders is probably the most important thing we can do to create shoulders that aren't chronically painful. This is accomplished through a variation of pulling exercises that strengthen the muscles on the back side of the shoulder. Examples include rows, rear delt flys, pull ups, deadlifts, etc.

    To create balance in shoulder strength, a general rule is to perform three times as many pull exercises as you do push.

3. **The Press**

    The press involves moving any amount of weight overhead. Extremely important for anyone who works overhead or athletes that repeatedly perform overhead (swimmers, volleyball players, gymnasts, etc) Examples include the overhead press, handstands, pikes, push press, etc.

When training these three movements, it's important to create balance. Because our push and press muscles are what we see in the mirror, many people over-train these movements, which can contribute to pain and injury.

The Perfect Push-Up

The push-up is one of the most common movements in which people get hurt in the fitness world, so we wanted to spend a little bit of time discussing the correct way to perform. For such a seemingly simple movement, the push-up has many variabilities and subtleties that need to be considered. Where we position our hands, elbows, feet and trunk all need to be considered to avoid the hot, burning pain in the front of our shoulders that is so often associated with the push-up. In this section we examine the proper positioning of our body in order perform the perfect push-up.

1. Hands

   As a rule, our hands need to be positioned directly under our shoulders. When in the lowered position your forearm should be close to vertical.

   Fingers need be aligned parallel to the body. It's common to see fingers turn out due to missing range of motion at the shoulder and wrist. This limits the amount of power we create as well as predisposes us to anterior shoulder and elbow pain.

2. Elbows

   Keep elbows close to the body. The most common compensation for missing shoulder range of motion is the elbows flaring out. This will always lead to wrist, elbow, or anterior shoulder pain if not corrected. In order to avoid the hot, burning pain in the front of your shoulders it's imperative to keep your elbows close to the body.

3. Trunk and Lower Body

An inability to maintain the plank position causes our butts to sag or be shot into the air. Both lead to injury and need to be avoided. Keeping your feet together helps activate the glutes which in turn creates stability in your trunk.

Keep in mind that fatigue becomes a huge factor when performing high volume push-ups. What starts as a perfect push-up easily becomes a sloppy and injury-prone push-up when programmed between other high-intensity exercises. Effort needs to be made to improve shoulder and core strength to perform the perfect push-up throughout the entirety of a workout.

Conclusion

We hope that you're starting to notice how all aspects of movement start to build on each other. Once we've mastered the basic movement patterns, we can begin to improve strength by simply adding resistance or adding an unstable surface. By making steady improvements through a progressive exercise plan we can protect our bodies from the repeated irritations caused by improper movement patterns and protect our joints through improved functional strength. This is how we help our clients get back to the activities they love so they can live their life without any limitations.

Chapter Nine
MOBILITY

People generally fall into one of two categories: too stiff or too mobile. In Chapter Nine we're focusing on those who are too stiff and need to improve the flexibility and mobility of their body.

Thinking all the way back to Chapter Two and our discussion of Regional Interdependence, we'll discuss how a lack of mobility in one area can lead to injury elsewhere in the body, and we'll revisit the alternating pattern of stability/mobility that exists in our body and how we can bring more mobility to the mid-back, hips, and ankle.

Compensation Patterns

We briefly discussed compensation patterns in Chapter Two, so we want to go into more detail here. Our bodies are smart. When we're limited in how we move, our body will compensate to perform the task at hand. These compensation patterns occur after an injury to protect an area (e.g. limping after a sprained ankle) or can be used to compensate for a lack of mobility. The low back is an easy example. We want our lower back to be stable and strong to prevent excess movement through our joints and intervertebral discs. If we're missing full mobility in our hips, our body will sacrifice some of its stability of the low back to obtain the full range of motion cause by our tight hips.

And herein lies the problem: **Compensation patterns only work for so long before something breaks down.** These compensations take loads off our weight-bearing joints and place them onto areas that weren't mean to carry such a load (like our low back). This causes wear and tear on these joints, and while you won't experience pain right away, the more miles you accumulate with these compensations the more likely you'll experience pain and dysfunction as well as increase the probability of experiencing a more serious injury later on down the road.

In general, the body has three areas we need to be sure stay mobile to avoid common compensation patterns. We'll cover them next.

Mid Back Mobility

Due to the demands of the modern human (e.g. long hours of sitting), one of the most common areas to lack mobility is the thoracic spine (or mid back).

An easy example is pictured on the right. To the left we have normal thoracic motion and you can see how the shoulders easily get into full flexion. The picture to the right is with the thoracic spine locked into flexion (typical of someone who works at a computer all day). Notice a difference in arm positioning?

Now imagine going into a fitness class with a lot of overhead movements. Or having to work long hours with your arms over your head (painting, anyone?). If you're unable to achieve full shoulder range of motion due to a lack of mid-back mobility, your shoulder muscles, ligaments, and tendons will eventually give out and lead to pain and injury.

Hip Mobility

The hip joint is made up of a "socket" on the pelvis (called the acetabulum) and a "ball" at the top of your thigh bone (femur), which we call the femoral head. Around the hip joint are a lot of muscles, a joint capsule, and connective tissue that help control the movement and stability of the hip. A loss of hip mobility will lead to a laundry list of compensations that will – over time – lead to pain and injury.

To give you a better idea of what we mean, we'll cover a few of the most common compensations that result from a lack of hip mobility. When we run, if we lack the ability to get our hip into full hip extension, our entire leg will turn outward to regain the missing range of motion. This puts more force on the knee and can also cause over-pronation of the foot. While the issue is poor hip mobility, the pain will be seen at the knees or feet.

When we squat, if we're missing full hip mobility the body will round our pelvis forward to achieve full depth (a term called the "butt wink"). This causes our spine to round forward and is an unstable position in which to be doing any sort of work. This may not be a problem with air squats, but the more repetitions or heavier weight we use put us at a higher risk for injury. Again, the issue is poor hip mobility, but we'll experience pain in the low back. This is why maintaining hip mobility and control is important in preventing pain/injury anywhere in the body.

Ankle Mobility

A lack of ankle movement is a common contributor to ankle, knee, hip, and back pain. The movement can be limited due to previous injuries, tight musculature (calves), restrictions in the joint itself, and even the shoes we wear.

While seemingly insignificant, limitations in ankle movement lead to a host of problems up the kinetic chain.

- A lack of dorsiflexion causes our trunk to lean forward during functional movements like the squat. This contributes to low back pain. This poor positioning can also inhibit performance in the gym and athletics by limiting our ability to generate power from the hips.

- A stiff foot is a foot that doesn't adequately absorb the forces of our daily life and therefore leads to increased forces being transferred up the kinetic chain. This is really bad for runners.

- This is why it's important for you to know how much ankle dorsiflexion you have and to identify strategies to improve it if you're lacking or if there's an imbalance side to side.

Self-Care Strategies

The Self-Care Techniques we discuss are hands-on techniques and exercises we use in the clinic to help clients self-manage pain and improve movement. None of these things are unique to our clinic and most are things you have probably heard of before, though we offer new and more effective approaches. We'll briefly discuss them here.

A New Approach to Foam Rolling

Just like anything in the pain and manual therapy world, the science is changing. What we thought we were accomplishing with traditional foam rolling happens to be wrong. Today we cover a more effective approach to foam rolling that saves time and pain.

Old Approach – Impacting the Muscular System

How foam rolling has been taught for the last 5 to 10 years is based on the idea that we can have an impact on lengthening the muscles themselves. The idea is that we're "breaking" adhesions in muscles that allow those muscles to lengthen. It turns out we need 2,000 pounds of pressure to cause any change in muscle length, making it impossible to accomplish with foam rolling.

But foam rolling has been an effective form of self-care for a long time, so what exactly are we doing?

<u>The New Approach – Impacting the Nervous System</u>

The new approach focuses on how we can affect the nervous system to create better range of motion in our muscles and joints. By gently rolling over our muscles we're stimulating the receptors in our skin and fascia (30% more receptors in our fascia vs. our muscles) to decrease the tone of that muscle. This decrease in tone allows for greater range of motion of targeted muscles and joints and is a great thing to add to any warm up routine.

How to Foam Roll More Effectively

With the idea that we're having a greater impact on the nervous system than we are on the muscles, we can now foam roll more effectively.

- **Time:** We no longer need to spend 1 to 2 minutes on each muscles group to "break the adhesion." We can lightly roll over the muscle group for 15 to 30 seconds and have the same effect.
- **Depth:** We also have no need to really dig into the muscles, which is often painful and uncomfortable. Lightly covering the muscles with our roller or tennis ball is enough to stimulate the nervous system to decrease the tone of our muscles.

Nerve Flossing

The peripheral nervous system is a continuous organ that runs throughout the entire body and can be injured through a variety of mechanisms including compression, traction, and friction. When the nerve tissue itself is injured it often causes a tingly, numbness sensation that can be felt anywhere along the course of the nerve. Compression can occur through a variety of mechanisms but is commonly associated with muscle shortening and tightness that physically puts pressure on your nerves.

The most common examples of this type of compression include carpal tunnel syndrome and thoracic outlet syndrome. When nerves do become impeded through restricted muscles and fascia, nerve flossing can be a great technique to break those adhesions in order to relieve numbness and tingling in your arm and fingers. Similar to flossing your teeth, the idea is to stretch your nerves through the surrounding muscles and fascia in order to break adhesions between the nerves and adjacent structures.

Dynamic Stretching

Just a reminder that STATIC stretching is not an effective self-care strategy. Dynamic stretching is a form of active movement that isn't about holding a stretch but rather taking your body through ranges of motion that will better prepare you for your workout or sporting activity.

Wrapping It All Up

We've reached the end of our journey. And just as we began, we'll end with a reminder to keep the big picture in mind: that improving movement and strength is less about overcoming pain and more about the impact that overcoming pain will have in your real life. It's about improving how you utilize the tools you were given to do what makes you happy. With that being said, the role of healthcare should aim to create the optimum conditions to achieve happiness.

With this definition, health becomes an action. Health is exploring. Health is competing. Health is spending time with family. It's about following your passion. It includes different lifestyles and body types while requiring the adoption of the lifestyle changes necessary to avoid the chronic pain and injury that could limit our ability to do what we love.

And that's what this book is about – how we can use movement and strength to not only get us out of pain, but to improve how we experience the world we live in.

Part Three

I bet at this point you're wondering, "But will this approach work for me?" Without knowing a single thing about you and your story, I can without a doubt say "YES." And I can say it with 100% confidence. How can I do that? **Because I know that there is no instance where improving movement and strength will not be beneficial in SOME aspect of your life. Where adopting a mindset of continual growth, learning, and confidence will not make you a better person and improve the quality of your life.**

In Part Three of this book we look at some case studies of individuals who have benefited from adopting this approach. I hope as you read through their stories you can relate to their stories, their worries and concerns, their hesitation to trying a new approach and it gives you hope. Hope that you aren't stuck with this annoying and nagging pain. Hope that you don't have to just sit and wait for it to get worse. And most importantly, that you don't have to be limited in the activities you can perform as you get older.

Chapter Ten
CASE STUDIES

Our clinic helps adults aged 40-plus stay moving and strong so they can keep up their lifestyle, do what they love, and live free of pain meds, endless treatments, and costly surgeries. As we end our discussion on the importance of movement and strength, we want to share some stories of the individuals we have helped with our unique combination of manual therapy with movement and strength therapy.

We want to share these stories because they are so common. When it comes to what you're going through, we can guarantee you that you are not alone. We have helped hundreds of people just like you get back to the activities they love and give them the tools to live their life without limitations-- even if nothing else has worked. You may find some similarities in these stories and we hope they can inspire you to take action.

Debbie – Late 50s – Portland, OR

Debbie, a grandmother and active runner, came to the clinic with chronic, left-sided hip pain. She is a very active runner, consistently signing up for 10Ks and half marathons. She was able to "run through" her hip pain for many years. By the time she came to our office the hip pain was so bad that it completely stopped her running routine.

During the course of care, we would hear phrases like, "I'm tired of having to always 'think' about my hip pain. Tired of having to 'think' about how to get in and out of the car. Tired of waking up every two hours because of pain. Tired of complaining to my husband."

Tired of dealing with hip pain and ready to make a change, Debbie committed to her treatment plan. We utilized some of our favorite manual therapy techniques to help heal the soft tissues surrounding the hip and got her started on a lower body strengthening/hip mobility routine. After only eight weeks, Debbie is back to her running routine and already signed up for her next half marathon!

Kristen – Late 30s – Portland, OR

Kristen presented to the clinic with bilateral knee pain of a three-year duration. Her pain had come on gradually and she had no previous fractures or surgeries in either leg. X-rays and MRIs showed two normal knees. But she still couldn't lunge, squat, or run without knee pain – a major problem for someone who loves to get outside and run and stay active in the gym. Before coming into the clinic, she had seen multiple providers and spent a lot of money only to find temporary relief that would come back when she stopped care. She was worried she would have to give up her fitness and running routine at such an early age. Because of her lack of long-term success, she was hesitant to commit to a full plan.

Her evaluation showed nothing positive in the "traditional knee exam." Nothing that suggested any sort of knee sprain, strain, or meniscus injury. Just pain. What we did find was an inefficiency in lower body and core strength along with side-to-side imbalances when it came to balance and strength in her legs.

"For years I was told I had 'bad knees' and I would never be able to run (or lunge, or squat) again. After 12 visits I am back in the gym and feel strong and more confident than before. I'm also back to running and just signed up for my first 5K in over three years!"

Curtis – Early 40s – Portland, OR

Curtis is a bartender, server, musician, and all-around great person. A very healthy and active person, he suffered a broken jaw after being randomly attacked while walking home. The jaw healed but it soon became infected and required surgery to fix. Even after the surgery his jaw consistently swelled up, causing lock jaw and shoulder pain that limited his ability to play music and enjoy his gym routine.

Curtis is one of the few clients who is so dedicated to his health that he consistently comes in for routine care. Working to improve jaw, neck, and shoulder function through movement pattern and strength training, he has seen a dramatic decrease in the frequency of jaw and shoulder pain. In the winter of 2018, he noticed that it was the first year he has been able to enjoy both Thanksgiving and Christmas meals without having lockjaw.

"I've been seeing Evolve for two months and my jaw and shoulder mobility and strength have improved immensely. I can now enjoy my two passions of

performing and exercises on a consistent and pain-free basis! Thanks Dr. Baird!"

Kristina – Early 50s – Portland, OR

Kristina is an active cyclist who has been putting up with aches and pains throughout her cycling and fitness journey. Cycling is more than a physical activity for her and is part of the way she feels connected to a community and relieves stress from her busy schedule. While her aches and pain were not yet debilitating, they were distracting, taking away from the enjoyment that she got from riding. She wanted to get back to being able to get 100% immersed in her cycling and fitness routines.

Putting a plan together to retrain her movement patterns and overall strength, she recently was able to complete the Cycle Oregon race pain free!

"After years of cycle training and putting up with aches and pains, I've discovered my patterns of movement just needed to be retrained! Evolve has enthusiastically and successfully helped me to live and pedal without pain (and what to do if...)! Thank you!"

Jared – Late 30s – Portland, OR

Jared is a dedicated runner. At the time he presented to the clinic he was in the midst of training for the World Marathon Challenge: a race that includes seven marathons, on seven continents, in seven days (yikes!). Relatively new to running he started to develop shin splints early on in his training. This was something he recognized would be a big problem as he increased his miles, and it needed to be addressed.

Similar to many runners we treat, his exam showed some side to side imbalances, hip mobility deficiencies, and leg strength deficiencies that, if corrected, would drastically improve his running performance. We worked with Jared to treat his shin splints, improve hip mobility, and strengthen his lower extremity so that he could support himself in the single leg stance. Because he had the foresight to seek help early, his shin splints went away within a few weeks. He stayed consistent with his strengthening program and successfully completed the World Marathon Challenge with no pain or injury (besides the expected aches and pains from running 182 miles in 7 days!).

"Working with Evolve helped me understand what it means to build a foundation for the body. This allowed me to take the work that we did in the clinic and apply it to the course."

Chapter Eleven

If you made it this far, I want to congratulate you first and foremost. We understand that not everyone is as passionate about movement as we are. We hope you gained a better understanding of how adding in a movement and strength program to your current healthcare routine is an absolutely crucial part to maintaining your active lifestyle and living your life without any limitations. The movement principles discussed in Part Two are basic, fundamental principles that can be used in any activity – from the workplace to the gym – and we hope you can find ways to incorporate them into your life to improve how you experience the world around you.

Our goal is to help you make the best decision for your health. If you've been dealing with pain that is limiting you from performing the activities you love, we would be happy to sit down and answer any of the concerning questions you may have. Here are a few of the ways you can set up an appointment to speak with a specialist for free.

Free 20-Minute Discovery Visit

We realize some people may be unsure if this type of care is right for them. Are you wondering whether it'll work, whether we can help with your problem, or maybe you've had a bad experience somewhere in the past? If that sounds like you and you'd like to come see for yourself how Evolve Performance Healthcare can help you, please send us an email or call to get started.

Free Phone Consultation

If you're not quite ready to book an appointment yet, you might have some questions that you would like answered first. Dr. Baird would be happy to chat with you so he can be 100% sure that he can help you. Send an email or call to schedule a time to talk.

Find Us on the Internet

- Website: www.performancehealthcarepdx.com
- Instagram: @performancehealthcarepdx
- Facebook: Evolve Performance Healthcare
- YouTube: https://www.youtube.com/EvolveChiropractic/

About the Author

Growing up an athlete continually hampered by injuries that limited his ability to enjoy and continue playing, Dr. Carl Baird has dedicated his career to helping active individuals stay moving and strong so they can keep up with their active lifestyle and avoid missing out on the activities they love. Frustrated by a healthcare system that places profits over patients, Dr. Baird opened Evolve Performance Healthcare in Portland, Oregon to provide an educational approach to medicine that empowers the patient to achieve SUSTAINABLE pain relief.

Every week for the past 10 years, Dr. Baird (and his pup Bandit) consults with hundreds of people looking for answers to their concerns regarding pain and injury. Along with his Doctorate of Chiropractic, Dr. Baird has earned his Masters of Science in Exercise Science and completed a post-graduate fellowship in sports medicine. His background in movement, fitness, and sports medicine gives him a unique perspective on the needs of the active individual and what it takes to maintain an active lifestyle.

He works with people aged 40 to 70 on a daily basis, teaching them how to overcome pain through better movement and increased functional strength. He is now founder of what is rapidly becoming one of the biggest private practices in the Portland area and the only one to offer customized care plans that combine the benefits of chiropractic care, manual therapy and therapeutic fitness plans to provide SUSTAINABLE pain relief — without the use of pain pills and endless doctor visits.

Be sure to connect with Dr. Baird on social media and let him know how this book has made an impact on you: @performancehealthcarepdx

About Evolve Performance Healthcare

Evolve Performance Healthcare was born out of a vision to deliver long-lasting results through expert, individualized healthcare combined with movement/functional fitness programs. Dr. Carl Baird worked for many years in busy, traditional chiropractic clinics and grew tired and frustrated with the over-reliance on adjustments and other passive therapies that left clients with short term relief— but no long-term solutions to their problems.

From this experience grew a passion to deliver high-level, one-on-one care that focuses on each client's unique passion and goals. We believe that health isn't something achieved in a doctor's office; it's something experienced in the real world. It is your ability to become 100% immersed in the activities you love — without pain distracting you from enjoying your life. With this vision in mind we aimed to create a clinic focused on helping people stay active and mobile while improving how they experience the world around them.

Made in the USA
Monee, IL
02 December 2020